CAREER CHOICES
FOR STUDENTS OF
BUSINESS

CAREER CHOICES
FOR THE
90's

FOR STUDENTS OF
BUSINESS

MOUNT ZION HIGH
MEDIA CENTER

WALKER AND COMPANY
NEW YORK

First published in the United States of America in 1990
by Walker Publishing Company, Inc.

Published simultaneously in Canada by Thomas Allen & Son
Canada, Limited, Markham, Ontario

Library of Congress Cataloging-in-Publication Data
Career choices for students of business / by Career Associates.
Includes bibliographical references.
ISBN 0-8027-7325-7
1. Vocational guidance—United States.   2. College graduates—
Employment—United States.   3. United States—Occupations.
4. Business—Vocational guidance—United States.   I. Career
Associates.
HF5382.5.U5C255   1990
331.7'023—dc20   89-70525
CIP

Printed in the United States of America

2 4 6 8 10 9 7 5 3 1

CAREER ASSOCIATES

ACKNOWLEDGMENTS

We gratefully acknowledge the help of the many people who spent time talking to our research staff about employment opportunities in their fields. This book would not have been possible without their assistance. Our thanks, too, to Catalyst, which has one of the best career libraries in the country in its New York, NY, offices, and to the National Society for Internships and Experiential Education, Raleigh, NC, which provided information on internship opportunities for a variety of professions.

We also acknowledge the contribution of the Financial Women's Association of New York, an organization composed of professionals from various industries, which helped us to locate some of the professionals interviewed in this book.

CONTENTS

What's in this book for you?

WHAT'S IN THIS BOOK FOR YOU?

With the 1990's in full force and the year 2000—the new millenium!—no longer a distant specter, it's more important than ever to look closely at the changes in different industries. Industries, and consequently, a student's career choices have changed dramatically in the last decade. This book is designed to give you the latest information on a range of different career possibilities.

Recent college graduates, no matter what their major has been, too often discover that there is a dismaying gap between their knowledge and planning and the reality of an actual career. Possibly even more unfortunate is the existence of potentially satisfying careers that graduates do not even know about. Although advice from campus vocational counselors, family, friends, and fellow students can be extremely helpful, there is no substitute for a structured exploration of the various alternatives open to graduates.

The Career Choices Series was created to provide you with the means to conduct such an exploration. It gives you specific, up-to-date information about the entry-level job opportunities in a variety of industries relevant to your degree and highlights opportunities that might otherwise be overlooked. Through its many special features—such as sections on internships, qualifications, and working conditions—the Career Choices Series can help you find out where your interests and abilities lie in order to point your search for an entry-level job in a productive direction. This book cannot find you a job—only you can provide the hard work, persistence, and ingenuity that that requires—but it can save you valuable time and energy. By helping you to narrow the range of your search to careers that are truly suitable for you, this book can help make hunting for a job an exciting adventure rather than a dreary—and sometimes frightening—chore.

The book's easy-to-use format combines general information about each of the industries covered with the hard facts that job-hunters must have. An overall explanation of each industry is followed by authoritative material on the job outlook for entry-level candidates, the competition for the openings that exist, and the new opportunities that may arise from such factors as expansion and technological development. There is a listing of employers by type and by geographic location and a sampling of leading companies by name—by no means all, but enough to give you a good idea of who the employers are.

Many young people are interested in being an entrepreneur and you'll find a section showing examples of people who have succeeded as entrepreneurs in the different industries. There's also a discussion of "intrapreneurship"—how you can be an entrepreneur within a large company.

The section on how to break into the field is not general how-to-get-a-job advice, but rather zeroes in on ways of getting a foot in the door of a particular industry.

You will find the next section, a description of the major functional areas within each industry, especially valuable in making your initial job choice. For example, communications majors aiming for magazine work can evaluate the editorial end, advertising space sales, circulation, or production. Those interested in accounting are shown the differences between management, government, and public accounting. Which of the various areas described offers you the best chance of an entry-level job? What career paths are likely to follow from that position? Will they help you reach your ultimate career goal? The sooner you have a basis to make the decision, the better prepared you can be.

For every industry treated and for the major functional areas within that industry, you'll learn what your duties—both basic and more challenging—are likely to be, what hours you'll work, what your work environment will be, and what range of salary to expect*. What personal and professional qualifications must you have? How can you move up—and to what? This book tells you.

---

*Salary figures given are the latest available as the book goes to press.

You'll learn how it is possible to overcome the apparent contradiction of the truism, "To get experience you have to have experience." The kinds of extracurricular activities and work experience—summer and/or part-time—that can help you get and perform a job in your chosen area are listed. Internships are another way to get over that hurdle, and specific information is included for each industry.

You'll find a list of the books and periodicals you should read to keep up with the latest trends in an industry you are considering, and the names and addresses of professional associations that can be helpful to you—through student chapters, open meetings, and printed information. Finally, interviews with professionals in each field bring you the experiences of people who are actually working in the kinds of jobs you may be aiming for.

Although your entry-level job neither guarantees nor locks you into a lifelong career path, the more you know about what is open to you, the better chance you'll have for a rewarding work future. The information in these pages will not only give you a realistic basis for a good start, it will help you immeasurably in deciding what to explore further on your own. So good reading, good hunting, good luck, and the best of good beginnings.

CAREER CHOICES
FOR STUDENTS OF
BUSINESS

ACCOUNTING

Ledger books, electronic spreadsheets, endless rows and columns of figures—a career spent with the tools of the accounting profession appeals to many business majors. With tax laws becoming more complicated and government regulations requiring more careful audits, the skills of the accountant are in greater demand than ever before.

Of course, the major tools of the accounting profession have undergone a tremendous change in the past decade or so, and those changes have in turn altered the nature of the profession to some degree. Electronic spreadsheets have at once made the accountant's work much less tedious and much more complex. Whereas before the dawn of the computer age an accountant might spend hours toting up and balancing a large spreadsheet on paper, now the appropriate numbers can be entered by keyboard into a package like Lotus 1-2-3, and within seconds all the calculations and totals are complete. The trade-off for this speed is that accountants generally have inherited more responsibility for seeking creative and alternative solutions to problems. The "what-if" business analysis is now a critical part of the accounting profession.

For this reason, a master of business administration is becoming increasingly relevant. Consider the fact that in the nation's major accounting firms, the biggest areas of growth are not in accounting but in management consulting. Obviously, anyone working for a major accounting firm must be numbers-savvy; increasingly, however, the major firms are looking for employees who also have a broader perspective on the business world.

Corporate America is also on the lookout for well-rounded business professionals with heavy accounting and financial analysis backgrounds. In most Fortune 500 companies, a chief financial officer is in place alongside the chief executive officer and the chief operating officer. In many cases, these CFOs have accounting backgrounds. Clearly, an M.B.A. degree could be a critical factor in any move to the executive suite.

The accounting profession is a large one, but most entry-level jobs are not suited to the skills gained through graduate work. Those employers who do seek candidates with advanced education will often hire a person with a master's in accounting over an M.B.A.

Whatever your background, you must demonstrate far more than fiscal and mathematical skills. Accountants do not work over their books in solitude; they are active participants in daily business operations. Their findings and observations must be used by others, so the would-be accountant must have exceptional organizational and communications skills. The ability to continue to learn is also a vital part of any accounting career because of ever changing tax laws and business regulations. Further education can also open up new career possibilities as your growing knowledge and experience allow you to explore new options.

Accounting professionals work in three major areas:

◆ **PUBLIC ACCOUNTING**

◆ **MANAGEMENT ACCOUNTING**

◆ **GOVERNMENT ACCOUNTING**

Public accounting is the most visible branch of the industry, primarily because of the status of the certified public accountant (C.P.A.). Public accountants serve client businesses by auditing their books, preparing tax returns, and advising on tax, business, investment, and related concerns. Management accountants, also known as private, internal, or industrial accountants, work within industries and businesses and with charitable, educational, and religious institutions. They handle such functions as cost analysis, budgeting, payroll, inventory control, and offer advice on financial matters. Government accountants perform the same role, but work within the government rather than in private industry.

Information processing technologies have significantly affected the daily routines of many accounting professionals. Computers are increasingly relied on for record-keeping and financial analysis. Accountants are now able to complete many jobs more quickly without sacrificing standards of thoroughness and accuracy.

JOB OUTLOOK

JOB OPENINGS WILL GROW: Faster than average

COMPETITION FOR JOBS: Keen

NEW JOB OPPORTUNITIES: The expanding, complex body of tax laws confronting the business community is creating an increased demand for tax accountants. Although most accountants do some tax work, larger businesses often need the services of accountants who specialize in this area. Job experience with the Internal Revenue Service (IRS) is the best education for anyone considering a career in tax accounting, but jobs in public and management accounting can also involve the newcomer in a great deal of tax work. If you are interested in this branch of the industry, be sure to study tax law and be aware of current changes in and additions to tax regulations.

GEOGRAPHIC JOB INDEX

New York, NY, Chicago, IL, Los Angeles, CA, and Washington, DC, have higher concentrations of accountants than other specific locales, but jobs are not limited to these cities. Accounting jobs may be found in all regions of the United States, mainly in urban and industrial areas.

WHO THE EMPLOYERS ARE

PUBLIC ACCOUNTING can mean working in a one-person operation or for an international giant employing thousands. According to the U.S. Department of Labor, about a third of the nation's nearly 950,000 accountants are Certified Public Accountants, and close to 10 percent of all accountants are self-employed. The most prestigious public accounting jobs are with the major accounting firms. These firms, formerly known as the Big Eight, are in the midst of continuing changes, with several mergers taking place between them.

MANAGEMENT ACCOUNTING in many businesses may require only one person handling some accounting functions, but the real career opportunities lie in large firms. You might also find work in service industries, such as hospitals and universities. Here you may work alone or with a small staff, and will be almost exclusively concerned with financial planning and analysis, rather than with the daily routine of basic accounting.

GOVERNMENT employs accounting staffs in departments and agencies at the federal, state, county, and municipal levels. Smaller governmental units, such as townships and boroughs, often hire public accounting firms to handle their books.

MAJOR EMPLOYERS

THE BIG ACCOUNTANCIES
Arthur Andersen & Co., Chicago, IL
Coopers & Lybrand, New York, NY
Deloitte Haskins & Sells/Touche Ross, New York, NY
Ernst & Young, Cleveland, OH
KPMG Peat Marwick, Montvale, NJ

Price Waterhouse & Co., New York, NY

These companies have branches throughout the country.

GOVERNMENT departments employing the largest numbers of accountants and auditors are:

Department of Agriculture
Department of Defense Audit Agencies
Department of Energy
Department of Health and Human Services
Department of the Air Force
Department of the Army
Department of the Navy
Department of Transportation
General Accounting Office
Treasury Department (includes the Internal Revenue Service)

HOW TO BREAK INTO THE FIELD

Because of keen competition for jobs with the major accounting firms, you need a strong grade point average and a high class standing. These firms recruit at business schools, as do other large employers of public accountants. However, because most public accounting firms do not have recruitment personnel, your best bet is to make your own investigation through personal referrals and newspaper advertisements.

Large businesses also recruit management accountants: Keep an eye on the classified ads and make direct applications to companies that interest you.

You must apply for government accounting jobs in the same way as for any other government job. At the federal level, contact the nearest job information center for application details. Most federal applicants must go through the Office of Personnel Management, but some departments, such as the Department of Defense, have their own personnel offices. In either case, you must submit the standard federal application form, SF-171, and a college transcript. Normally, the federal government promotes from within, but occasionally openings appear that cannot be filled without looking for outside talent. After your application is received, your qualifications are evaluated and you are given a numerical rating. When your number reaches the head of a list of qualified candidates for the position that interests you, you will be interviewed. If the job is in another part of the country and you are willing to relocate—always an important consideration when applying for federal work—you may be interviewed on the phone.

Application requirements with smaller government bodies vary. Contact state, county, or local government personnel agencies to learn their needs for applicants with advanced degrees.

INTERNATIONAL JOB OPPORTUNITIES

The largest public accounting firms and corporations have overseas branches, but these are staffed by foreign nationals in most areas. An exception is the Middle East, where Americans who are fluent in Arabic are needed.

ENTREPRENEURIAL

The accounting profession seems tailor-made for individuals imbued with the entrepreneurial spirit. Nearly 100,000 accountants in the United States are self-employed, and many others are proprietors of small independent firms.

Clearly, these numbers suggest that the possibility to succeed as a self-employed accountant exists. They also suggest, however, that the competition among entrepreneurial accountants is stiff. Setting up your own accounting practice may not take a lot of money—you can work out of your own home, and aside from a microcomputer there isn't much equipment you need to invest in—but it does take a lot of patience and perseverance.

In many cases, it also takes C.P.A. certification. Experts agree that certified public accountants are in greater demand by those small companies that are most likely to hire self-employed accountants. When it comes to setting up your own business C.P.A. certification is an impressive track record at a large firm.

A few accounting experts have taken advantage of their specialized knowledge, and the general public's phobias concerning numbers ad taxes, to start lucrative careers in the writing business. The business sections of book stores are filled with self-help books and insider's guides to filling out tax returns, starting your own business, and managing your financial assets. Many of these books are written by experienced accountants. As tax laws continue to change and grow more complex—and as more Americans try to strike out on their own in business endeavors—book publishers are sure to be beating the bushes for do-it-yourself accounting books and manuals.

PUBLIC ACCOUNTING

The most important function of the public accountant is auditing. This includes an inspection of the client's internal operations, records, documents, and possibly, company employees on the job. The auditor inspects procedures for bill paying, inventory control, and other financial operations and establishes the balances of income, debts, assets, and investments. Auditors base their final reports on their observations, experience, and knowledge of sound business practices. A background in economics and business administration is valuable in this respect. Auditors must also be able to exercise good judgment.

The audit gives clients a complete and accurate assessment of their financial standing. It aids management in planning and protects investors and stockholders. An annual audit is mandatory for all publicly held corporations.

Many businesses and organizations, even those with internal accounting departments, hire public accountants to prepare tax returns. These clients see a distinct advantage in having an objective agency perform this important task. In such cases, the public accountant adopts the role of tax adviser.

Some businesses also engage public accountants to provide advice on investments and accounting procedures, performing for small firms the same functions as internal accountants in larger businesses.

Certified public accountants receive greater recognition than other public accountants, both from the public and from other account professionals. You are awarded certification once you have demonstrated your mastery of accounting skills in a five-part examination. The exam tests accounting theory, commercial law, and accounting techniques. A standard national test is used, but it is administered by state boards of accountancy, which may set their own requirements. All sections of the test need not be taken in one sitting, and any sections not passed may be retaken. The time period in which you must pass the complete exam varies from state to state. Some states also require a minimum amount of work experience as a public accountant before awarding the certificate. To check the standards of the state in which you plan to practice, consult that state's board of accountancy or the American Institute of Certified Public Accountants (AICPA).

To begin preparing for the exam while still in school, pay particular attention to courses in accounting theory. This material is learned only in an academic environment. Many C.P.A.s recommend that this section be taken first, before your classroom knowledge is obscured by time.

Having a C.P.A. is advantageous. It serves as tangible proof of your skill and your commitment to the profession. Public accounting firms, particularly the largest, often expect their accountants to receive certification as quickly as state law allows.

Beyond the entry level, the C.P.A. is often a requirement for advancement. Employers, even those in management and government accounting, prefer to see a C.P.A. when hiring an individual with public accounting experience. In private industry, C.P.A.s tend to be better paid than their noncertified counterparts. Although a varied career is possible without the certificate, having it opens a multitude of otherwise unavailable opportunities.

In most large public accounting firms, you begin your job with a formal training period, generally a few weeks, to acquaint yourself with your employer's standards and practices. Only some 2 percent of those hired as staff accountants reach the level of partner, so if you get to be a partner you are joining a select group of people who have the ability to be both good accountants and good administrators.

QUALIFICATIONS

PERSONAL: Good concentration. Patience. Accuracy and attention to detail. Flexibility. Objectivity. Ability to judge and make decisions. Reliability.

PROFESSIONAL: Writing and communications skills. Exceptional mathematical ability. Commitment to professional standards. Ability to work independently.

CAREER PATHS

LEVEL	JOB TITLE	EXPERIENCE NEEDED
Entry	Staff or junior accountant	Work experience often preferred
2	Senior accountant	1–3 years
3	Manager	3–5 years
4	Partner	8+ years

JOB RESPONSIBILITIES ◆ ENTRY LEVEL

THE BASICS: Preparing a client's books. Performing transactional tests (these verify the accuracy of bookkeeping procedures). Preparing tax returns.

MORE CHALLENGING DUTIES: Offering your recommendations and opinions on sections of an audit to senior personnel. Doing background research. Learning tax law. Meeting with clients.

MOVING UP

Promotion in any size firm depends on your competence in accounting techniques and procedures. Senior accountants are responsible for the transactional tests that ensure the accuracy of your findings. At the entry level you may be asked your opinion of an audit's findings, but only experienced personnel report directly to a client. Managers oversee the largest audits and service clients. The partners are the owners/executives of a public accounting firm, and are ultimately responsible for all decisions concerning the firm and its clients. They also solicit new accounts. You must be invited to become a partner and, in some cases, may have to buy into the firm.

Solo practice is an option open to experienced accountants. The advantage of working alone or starting your own small firm is that you may be selective in your choice of accounts. However, only a highly organized individual can successfully handle solo practice.

MANAGEMENT ACCOUNTING

Management accountants handle internal financial record-keeping. They provide data on investments, taxes, budgets, and cost analysis, and aid executive personnel in financial decision-making. These duties sound similar to those of public accountants with good reason—many businesses employ public accountants only to conduct audits; in-house staff handle all other accounting functions. Other organizations divide their accounting needs between public and management accounting, giving some functions, such as taxes, to an outside firm and assign day-to-day jobs, such as payroll and budgeting, to the internal staff. For this reason, the career paths and duties of management accountants vary considerably.

The general accounting department handles daily business needs, such as payroll, budgeting, accounts receivable, accounts payable, general ledger, and financial statements. In smaller firms, the title general accountant might be held by the individual who handles or directs most or all accounting functions. This individual would, in turn, work most closely with public accountants if the organization employs them.

General accountants must pay close attention to all laws and regulations affecting daily business operations. They are involved in sending out all payments, royalties, dividends, rents, and other necessary expenditures. General accountants also offer advice on affordability of purchases and services.

Tax accountants prepare tax returns and must be extremely knowledgeable about federal, state, and local tax laws. For this reason, many tax accountants have prior experience in public or government accounting. Senior accountants are responsible for seeing that the organization conforms to all tax laws.

Cost accountants determine the cost of goods and services. Their work is needed by manufacturing and service industries alike. They are instrumental in determining prices that are high enough to ensure a profit but low enough to interest consumers. Cost accountants work with marketing and manufacturing staffs, and some familiarity with the work of these departments is helpful.

Internal auditing is a specialized area of management accounting that has attracted a great deal of interest in recent years. Because of the growing body of federal legislation concerning business accounting standards and public access to information about corporate finances, internal auditing has changed from the luxury it once was to an absolute necessity. The internal auditor conducts an independent appraisal from within the organization by analyzing, criticizing, and recommending improvements to internal financial practices. The internal auditor also ensures the safety and profitability of investments and assets, and seeks to uncover sources of waste and inefficiency. By virtue of being inside the organization, the internal auditor is privy to confidential information that is not shared with auditing public accountants.

In addition to being a skilled accountant, the internal auditor must have a comprehensive understanding of all fundamental business areas: marketing, manufacturing, advertising, and stockholder relations. Internal auditing is an excellent path to an executive position because of the background provided by this exposure. However, despite the thrill of investigation, internal auditing is largely a job of long hours and repetitive work. One must be an individual of exceptional diligence and concentration.

An M.B.A. is a requirement for going into a specialized area of management accounting—financial planning and analysis. Financial planners are concerned with the budgetary and financial needs of an organization, investigating expenditures, profits, cash flow, and investments. They offer financial advice on the effects of mergers and corporate growth and may have the power to reject or discourage major expenditures and investments.

The management accounting end of the industry is aware of the need to demonstrate a commitment to high professional standards. Certification is now available to management accountants: the Certificate in Management Accounting (C.M.A.) and the Certified Internal Auditor (C.I.A.). The C.M.A. exam is sponsored by the National Association of Accountants and tests decision-making capability and knowledge of business law, finance, and organization. The C.I.A. exam is sponsored by the Institute of Internal Auditors and tests the theory and practice of internal auditing. Work experience is required for certification. Multiple certification is permissible and encouraged.

QUALIFICATIONS

PERSONAL: Reliability. Ability to work independently. Flexibility. Discipline.

PROFESSIONAL: Understanding of business and the marketplace. Willingness to increase your knowledge of practical accounting techniques.

CAREER PATHS

LEVEL	JOB TITLE	EXPERIENCE NEEDED
Entry	Staff accountant	Work experience often preferred
2	Senior accountant	1–3 years
3	General accountant, manager of tax accounting, cost analysis, etc., chief internal auditor	4–8 years
4	Treasurer, controller, chief financial officer	10+ years

JOB RESPONSIBILITIES ♦ ENTRY LEVEL

THE BASICS: Bookkeeping. Writing and recording checks. Filling out tax returns. Keeping files.

MORE CHALLENGING DUTIES: Offering your ideas on improved accounting procedures. Helping to prepare reports on company finances. Learning about the accounting department's relationship with other sections of the organization.

MOVING UP

From the beginning you must demonstrate your understanding of basic accounting techniques and an ability to handle the assignments given you. Mastering the various functions of your department, and understanding that department's place in the accounting structure is vital. Your responsibilities include preparing reports and analyses of your work which will be done under the aegis of a senior accountant. As you gain experience you may handle large or unusual transactions, and become involved in financial planning. As a manager you are involved with the entire organization, not just the accounting department.

The controller is the executive in charge of all accounting functions and summarizes financial information for executive personnel. This individual must have a keen understanding of all business operations and the judgment to make financial planning decisions. The treasurer handles the cash flow and all financial reserves and is involved with loans, credit, and investments. Many firms combine the functions of controller and treasurer into one position.

The chief financial officer oversees the controller, treasurer, chief internal auditor, and the accounting staffs. He or she advises top executives as to the financial needs and stability of the organization. The chief financial officer does not have to be an accountant, but often this individual has accounting experience. That top financial management can rise from the ranks of accountants demonstrates the importance of the accounting department in overall policy-making.

GOVERNMENT ACCOUNTING

Government accounting attracts those graduates and experienced accountants who want to use the skills of management accounting in a different setting. Government agencies tend to pay less than private industry, but as an employer, government offers distinct advantages: job security, excellent benefits, and some unique opportunities. The goal of the accounting department of a typical government agency is to function within the budgetary constraints mandated by legislative action. If government service interests you, keep in mind that it is primarily the federal government, which offers some unique options, that will want you, not state or local governments.

The IRS is the single largest employer of accountants in the United States. The IRS particularly needs accounting graduates to be agents—the people on the receiving end of federal tax returns. This job requires strong accounting abilities and the temperament to work with taxpayers.

IRS work requires extensive entry-level training. You being with an orientation and seven weeks of classroom training covering all aspects of tax law, fraud examination, and research techniques. Then, under the guidance of professionals, you continue your training on the job by reviewing simple taxpayer returns. Next, you receive classroom training on the examination of corporate tax returns and work with such returns. Finally, you are instructed in handling the more complex corporate returns, learning about tax shelters and other intricacies of tax law.

As you progress, you might remain a tax generalist, specialize in the returns of a particular industry, or be called on to instruct new trainees. Investigations or special projects might also require your participation.

The SEC offers excellent opportunities for experienced C.P.A.s who have at least three years of experience working with publicly held corporations in a public accounting firm. The SEC regulates all firms that sell stock by developing general accounting and auditing regulations and reviewing such companies' compliance with these regulations. After analyzing an audit of a particular corporation, the SEC may call for an investigation.

The army has centralized its accounting staff at the United States Army Finance Accounting Center, located at Fort Benjamin Harrison in Indianapolis, IN. Job openings exist for both operations accountants, who handle daily accounting needs, and systems accountants, who develop computer-based accounting systems for military bases and offices. Once you are employed by the federal government, you can transfer to other departments and agencies. You may move to a similar position, or to one with greater responsibilities. Current employees ("status employees," as they are called) receive preference in all hiring decisions.

Opportunities at state and local levels vary, but the greatest need for accountants is normally found in the larger departments and agencies, such as those handling transportation and road maintenance, law enforcement, and tax collection.

ADDITIONAL INFORMATION

SALARIES

Salaries vary according to the employer's size. The following salary ranges for starting annual salaries are taken from Robert Half International's most recent study. Holders of a C.P.A. will earn approximately 10 percent more than their peers who lack certification. At the managerial level, earnings will be reduced by about 5 percent for non-C.P.A.s.

PUBLIC ACCOUNTING

Entry level	$20,000 to $23,000 (medium-size firm)
	$22,000 to $25,500 (large firm)
1–3 years experience	$22,000 to $28,000 (medium)
	$23,500 to $28,000 (large)
Senior	$28,000 to $38,000 (medium)
	$28,000 to $32,000 (large)
Supervising senior	$32,000 to $38,000 (usually large firms only)
Manager	$38,000 to $52,000 (medium)
	$38,500 to $60,000 (large)

MANAGEMENT ACCOUNTING

Entry level	$18,500 to $22,000 (medium-size firm)
	$20,000 to $24,000 (large firm)
1–3 years experience	$25,000 to $31,000 (medium)
	$27,000 to $33,600 (large)
Senior	$32,500 to $40,300 (medium)
	$35,000 to $43,000 (large)
Manager	$40,500 to $50,000 (medium)
	$43,750 to $53,750 (large)

GOVERNMENT ACCOUNTING

Government accountants are paid according to standard pay scales. For federal salaries, consult the Office of Personnel Management for current figures.

WORKING CONDITIONS

HOURS: Accounting is a nine-to-five job, except during tax season. The workload during this period—roughly December to May—is especially heavy for public accountants and tax accountants. Expect long hours, weekend work, and no time off.

ENVIRONMENT: Accounting is an office job, but surroundings vary from employer to employer. At the entry level you might share an office, have a desk in a general work area, or at large businesses and public accounting firms, enjoy the luxury of a private office from the beginning. As you progress, your surroundings become more comfortable. Management accountants work in the administrative offices of their organizations. As an accountant for the Department of Defense, you might work as a civilian on a military base.

WORKSTYLE: Most work is done at your desk, but public accountants frequently work at clients' offices. Management and government accountants generally have fewer opportunities to work out of the office.

TRAVEL: Travel opportunities exist for many accounting professionals. Even in small public accounting firms, overnight travel may be required for visits to clients. In large firms you might spend days or weeks away on a single project. In management accounting, internal auditing staffers are most likely to travel; in multinational corporations this can mean international travel for experienced personnel. Certain federal departments, such as the Department of Defense, require extensive national and international travel.

RECOMMENDED READING

BOOKS
Accounting Principles, 15th ed., by Philip E. Fess and Carl S. Warren, South-Western Publishing: 1987

The Accounting Wars by Mark Stevens, Macmillan Publishing Company: 1985

A Reference Guide to Essentials of Accounting by Robert Newton Anthony, Addison-Wesley: 1985

Financial Accounting: An Introduction to Concepts, Methods, and Uses, 4th ed., by Sidney Davidson, Clyde P. Stickney, and Roman L. Weil, Dryden Press: 1985

PERIODICALS

Accounting Horizons and *Accounting Review* (both quarterly), American Accounting Association, 5717 Bessie Drive, Sarasota, FL 34233

CPA Journal (monthly), New York Society of Certified Public Accountants, 200 Park Avenue, New York, NY 10166

Government Accountants Journal (quarterly), Association of Government Accountants, 601 Wythe Street, Alexandria, VA 22314

The Internal Auditor (monthly), Institute of Internal Auditors, 249 Maitland Avenue, Altamonte Springs, FL 32715

Journal of Accountancy (monthly), American Institute of Certified Public Accountants, 1211 Avenue of the Americas, New York, NY 10036

Management Accounting (monthly), National Association of Accountants, 10 Paragon Drive, Montvale, NJ 07645

The National Public Accountant (monthly), National Society of Public Accountants, 1010 North Fairfax Street, Alexandria, VA 22314

The Practical Accountant (monthly), Warren, Gorham, and Lamont, Inc., One Penn Plaza, New York, NY 10119

The Wall Street Journal (daily), 200 Burnett Road, Chicopee, MA 01021

The Woman CPA (quarterly), American Society of Women Accountants and American Women's Society of Certified Public Accountants, 35 East Wacker Drive, Chicago, IL 60601

PROFESSIONAL ASSOCIATIONS

American Accounting Association
5717 Bessie Drive
Sarasota, FL 34233

American Institute of Certified Public Accountants
1211 Avenue of the Americas
New York, NY 10036

American Society of Women Accountants
35 East Wacker Drive
Chicago, IL 60601

Association of Government Accountants
601 Wythe Street
Alexandria, VA 22314

Institute of Internal Auditors
249 Maitland Avenue
Altamonte Springs, FL 32715

National Association of Accountants
10 Paragon Drive
Montvale, NY 07645

National Society of Public Accountants
1010 North Fairfax Street
Alexandria, VA 22314

INTERVIEWS

RICHARD N. LEMIEUX
PARTNER
ERNST & YOUNG
CLEVELAND, OH

The business environment has always fascinated me—even in high school I kept abreast of the stock market and corporate activity—so naturally, I studied business administration in college. I was interested in a career that would be different from the usual nine-to-five routine, a profession that would provide challenge and opportunity. An internship with a Big Eight accounting firm convinced me that public accounting was a profession that I would enjoy.

The combination of a master's degree (M.B.A.) and the internship experience gave me a distinct advantage in the job market. It enabled me to start my career with Ernst & Young at a step above the entry-level position. I obtained my C.P.A certificate and began to pursue a long-term goal of partnership.

The public accounting environment has more than met my expectations for a rewarding career. Although the hours may be demanding at times, I enjoy the travel, the variety of engagements and special projects, and the dedicated people in the firm. After fifteen years with E&Y I can honestly say I enjoy every new day.

Presently, I am in Ernst & Young's national office in Cleveland, Ohio. This is an opportunity that has allowed me to transfer from our Portland, Maine, office to work in an environment that is different from anything I thought I'd be doing—working in the internal managerial functions of the firm. Specifically, I am serving as partner in charge of personnel administration, dealing mostly with the administration of personnel policy, corporate relocation, recruiting, and human resource information systems. I am also involved with the Ernst & Young Foundation, which is responsible for the firm's matching gift program and grants to colleges and universities.

Careers in public accounting present challenges that are not always associated with accounting. For example, many of our audit staff are developing more responsive and efficient audit approaches with the use of microcomputer applications. Our tax professionals are constantly involved in new tax research and legislation, and our consultants are continuously expanding our information systems capabilities.

In summary, the public accounting profession offers unlimited challenges!

CATHERINE A. V. YAXLEY, CPA, MBA
SUPERVISOR
COOPERS & LYBRAND
NEW YORK, NY

The core courses within the standard undergraduate accounting program are accompanied by business courses intended as a supplement to the accounting curriculum. The M.B.A. in Public Accounting, however, provides a comprehensive foundation for understanding the business and financial environment, and enables one to view business situations not only from the necessarily detailed perspective of specific transactions and their implications, but from the broad based businessperson's vantage point as well.

Of the many employment opportunities an M.B.A. might consider, public accounting—and in particular, auditing—provides an ideal environment for developing and fine tuning these abilities. From a purely practical standpoint, auditing provides the experience required for certification as a C.P.A. A number of accounting majors enter public accounting firms with the goal of completing this requirement and "moving on" to private industry. The advantages offered by the C.P.A. firm are forsaken for the more limited experience of a single company.

In private industry, the tendency is to be hired to focus on one particular area within the firm. While the individual does become expert within that area, it is unlikely that he or she will develop an overall expertise as regards the company as a whole. Similarly, the concentration within a single area generally does not force the person to acquire an in-depth understanding of the industry and its economic, political, and social environment.

In public accounting, learning is achieved through resolution of complex and unusual business situations and transactions, exposure to diverse companies and industries, and interaction with clients and peers. The environment is, understandably, fast paced and demanding. It is also challenging and highly conducive to personal and professional growth.

Public accounting offers tremendous opportunities to the person who wishes to, and who is able to progress rapidly. Promotions are based upon professional readiness rather than corporate vacancies, thus enabling an individual to progress at his or her own pace. Levels of responsibility likewise increase as fast as one is able to assume them. Even the person who ultimately decides not to remain in public accounting acknowledges the fact that extensive employment opportunities are available to the person with public accounting experience.

Those M.B.A.s who decide to enter public accounting are faced with the question of working with a "Big Eight" versus a smaller C.P.A. firm. Given its larger resources, a Big Eight generally is able to provide a much broader experience. This writer's professional experience at Coopers & Lybrand, one of the largest of the Big Eight, has included domestic and international clients within such varied industries as consumer products, advertising, mining, and environmental protection.

In addition to auditing experience, the large firms are also equipped to offer more in the way of non-audit experience. Given their comprehensive and competitive approach to business, large firms need to have full consulting, information systems, actuarial, mergers and acquisitions and other services, in addition to the traditional auditing and taxation specialties. For the person eager to have a varied experience, exposure to more than one department greatly increases the individual's overall effectiveness from both a business as well as technical perspective. Again, this writer's experience at Coopers & Lybrand has included time spent not only in audit, but in the tax and mergers and acquisitions areas as well.

There is much truth to the statement that public accounting is not for everyone. Before an informed decision to enter the profession can be made, a thorough assessment of one's aspirations and abilities must be made. For the person who wishes to progress rapidly and who truly thrives in a challenging, non-routine environment, public accounting will undoubtedly prove itself to be a medium for growth and satisfaction—personally, professionally, and financially.

ADVERTISING

Are you someone who spends as much time looking at the ads in a magazine as at the articles themselves? Do you resist the urge to change channels when a commercial comes on so that you can see how companies are hawking their wares? Are you as interested in finding out who won a Clio as who won an Oscar or a Tony? If your answer to these questions is yes, or even if you know what a Clio is, chances are you're a good candidate for a career in advertising.

It's fairly common knowledge that a career in advertising is not for the faint of heart. The pace on Madison Avenue is fast, faster, fastest, and an agency's resident genius of a month ago can find himself or herself out of a job tomorrow. Winning a new account brings hearty praise and rich rewards. Losing a lucrative client often means a trip to the unemployment line. Advertising professionals have to know what's hot, what's happening—and what's on the way out.

For the past few years, this sort of instability has infected not only the individuals who work for advertising agencies but also the agencies themselves. As in other businesses, merger and buy-out mania has gripped the ad agency business, as agencies seek to gain the upper hand in the global economy and impress important clients with their sheer size. Size, however, isn't always an asset, a lesson that some mega-agencies like Saatchi & Saatchi and J. Walter Thompson have learned in recent years. Clients, no matter how large or small, demand the utmost attention from their agencies, no matter how large or small. When they don't get that attention, they take their business elsewhere.

Advertising agencies hire people from a wide variety of backgrounds—liberal arts, communications, business, and psychology among them—because jobs requiring different skills exist in the four major departments:

◆ **CREATIVE**

◆ **MEDIA**

◆ **RESEARCH**

◆ **ACCOUNT SERVICES**

At most agencies, the greatest number of jobs can be found in the creative department, where ads are written (and designed by people with a visual arts background) and the media department, which deals with planning a marketing strategy and buying air time and space in printed media for the agency's ads. As a copywriter, your communications or English degree will matter less than your actual speaking and writing skills. It is important to be an idea person, able to come up with many approaches to describe a product. If you want to go into media, ease with numbers is a must.

Research, which studies consumers' perceptions of products and advertising effectiveness, also hires entry-level people from a variety of disciplines, although a solid statistical background is a real asset. You must be able to read and interpret data, and have a real interest in the products and consumer reactions to them.

Account Services, where people work hand-in-hand with the clients, is reserved for those who have already gained experience in the industry. It's the most direct link with clients and a path to management positions. The media department is the surest route to the account group, although some researchers end up there as well.

Some large agencies rotate promising candidates through the media, research, and traffic departments on the way to account services.

Although there is good money to be made in advertising at big agencies, the advertising industry offers less security than many media professions. When an agency loses a major client, those who worked on that account are often let go. If enough income is lost, additional cuts may be made in areas not directly involved. Because client satisfaction is paramount, everyone who works at an agency—from top management to department heads to assistants—feels the pressure of getting work out when the client requests it. That often means staying late to make sure that the copy or reports or recommendations are the best job possible given the time constraints the client has set.

Technological advances are helping to increase the advertising industry's efficiency and organization. Microcomputers are now a standard piece of equipment in all agency departments, from research and billing to creative. Facsimile technology seems tailor-made for the advertising profession. Agencies can now send sketches to clients around the world in a matter of minutes.

JOB OUTLOOK

JOB OPENINGS WILL GROW: As fast as average

COMPETITION FOR JOBS: Keen

NEW JOB OPPORTUNITIES: As long as businesses and entrepreneurs have products and services to sell, they will need advertising professionals to help mold and hone their sales pitches. One of the faster-growing advertising segments is in the cable TV market. Smaller businesses that cannot afford to buy air time on over-the-air stations are finding cable TV advertising to be relatively inexpensive and effective. As the cable industry grows even larger in the coming years, the number of advertisers requiring agency services should grow.

GEOGRAPHIC JOB INDEX

New York, NY, is the home of major ad agencies, the headquarters of the media and many Fortune 500 firms, many of which also have advertising departments of their own. Chicago, IL, Los Angeles, CA, and Detroit, MI, are the next largest advertising centers. The advertising industry is growing faster than average in Atlanta, GA, Dallas, TX, and Houston, TX.

WHO THE EMPLOYERS ARE

ADVERTISING AGENCIES in the United States number than 6000. Nearly all major advertising is created within agencies, where the vast majority of jobs are. Most agencies are small, but about a third are large organizations, some employing more than 1000 people.

IN-HOUSE AGENCIES can be found at large companies. In-house agencies provide anything from specialized functions to the full range of marketing services, some of which exceed what full-service agencies offer. Packaged-goods companies rely on independent agencies for most of their work, with the exception of TV network placement. Although responsibilities and salaries are comparable to those in independent agencies, there is less competition for creative jobs in corporate environments.

MAJOR EMPLOYERS

Backer Spielvogel Bates Worldwide Inc., New York, NY
BBDO Worldwide Inc., New York, NY
D'Arcy Masius Benton & Bowles Inc., New York, NY
Doyle Dane Bernbach International Inc., New York, NY
Foote, Cone & Belding, Chicago, IL
J. Walter Thompson Company, New York, NY
Leo Burnett Company Inc., Chicago, IL
Lintas Worldwide, New York, NY
McCann-Erickson Worldwide, New York, NY

Ogilvy & Mather Worldwide Inc., New York, NY
Saatchi & Saatchi Worldwide Inc., New York, NY
Young & Rubicam Inc., New York, NY

HOW TO BREAK INTO THE FIELD

Talent, persistence, assertiveness, and enthusiasm are particularly important ingredients in the job campaign of a would-be ad person. If you cannot creatively and imaginatively sell yourself, chances are you won't be good at selling ideas and products to the public—and employers are quick to sense that.

Large agencies are often in contact with the placement directors at a select number of colleges, so it pays to check with that office on your campus. Large companies with their own in-house agencies sometimes recruit on college campuses. More often than not, it will be up to you to set up interviews on your own. Find out all you can about the agencies at the top of your list (alumni who work there are often good sources of information).

To land a job in the creative department, you need a portfolio of your writing and ideas. It can include your best work on the school paper or radio or TV station. It's less important that your work was published or used commercially than that it shows originality and imagination.

While portfolios aren't necessary for jobs in the other three major departments, sensitivity to and interest in contemporary tastes and trends, and some knowledge of the various media are.

INTRAPRENEURIAL

There's no question that the biggest money in advertising is at the biggest agencies. Starting salaries at the big agencies can be $10,000 to $15,000 higher than at smaller firms. At a large outfit your chances are better of working on an exciting, big-name account, seeing your work light up the screen on prime-time network TV, or occupy that choice space in *Time* or *Newsweek*.

If you really want to learn the ins and outs of the advertising business, everything from creative to account work to administration, the place to cut your teeth is at a smaller agency. A typical small firm may include a dozen or so staffers, including the partners. With such a small staff, the division of labor is sure to be quite different than at a larger firm, where copywriters are copywriters and assistant production managers are assistant production managers.

At a small agency, there's little chance of being pigeon-holed. You're likely to work on everything the agency handles: print ads, direct marketing campaigns, broadcast ads, billboards, you name it. The pressure to perform is no less intense at a small agency. In fact, the loss of a single client can be devastating to a tiny firm. You can be sure that you will have a definite impact on the agency's success or failure—and if it's a success, you will certainly be noticed.

CREATIVE

Writing copy requires a feeling for the language that goes beyond the simple communication of information. Rhythm, syntax, and meaning influence the choice of words that will create the right mood and reaction. Copywriters are well paid for their talent, since their command of the language can move millions to purchase a product. In fact, television commercial copywriters earn more money per word than any other kind of writer.

The best way to break into any agency—large or small—is to show that you're a good idea person who is able to come up with clever phrases, catchy slogans, and eye-catching copy. As a junior copywriter, you will be working as a member of a creative team under the supervision of a more experienced copywriter. You may be expected to write copy for a campaign, or you may have to come up with some original ideas for selling a product or service. Depending on the size of the agency and the importance of the campaign, you may be invited to take part in brainstorming sessions, where a group of creative people toss out ideas for a new campaign.

QUALIFICATIONS

PERSONAL: Good interpersonal skills. A good imagination. Persuasiveness. A strong enough ego to withstand frequent criticism. Sensitivity to current trends. Enormous enthusiasm. Ability to work under pressure.

PROFESSIONAL: Strong language and writing skills. Knowledge of the media.

CAREER PATHS

LEVEL	JOB TITLE	EXPERIENCE NEEDED
Entry	Junior copywriter	College degree
2	Copywriter	1–3 years
3	Senior copywriter	7–10 years
4	Copy chief	10 + years

JOB RESPONSIBILITIES ♦ ENTRY LEVEL

THE BASICS: Learning about the client or clients from printed material and past correspondence. In small agencies: Answering the phone. Typing. Filing. Drafting simple correspondence.

MORE CHALLENGING DUTIES: Writing descriptive copy. Coming up with concepts for new ad campaigns. Working with the art department on presentations.

MOVING UP

Your success will be linked to the success of your creative group at a large agency; at a small one, your effectiveness depends directly on your own contribution. Promotions will be based on your consistently good ideas and great copy. Moving up may mean getting a more significant role to play on a national account or being switched to a more prestigious client. With several years' experience and a solid track record, you may become a supervisor of other copywriters and work with the media and account groups developing ad campaign concepts.

MEDIA

A sound strategy for the placement of ads is the job of media planners, who must reduce quantities of raw numerical material to arrive at the most cost-effective way of reaching potential buyers.

As an assistant, you'll be assigned to work on an account under the supervision of a more experienced planner. In big agencies, as many as 25 to 30 people from the four major groups (account, creative, research, and media) may be involved in the media planning process, although you'll work primarily with the account services people. Developing a media strategy involves studying the target audience, geography (where customers live), seasonality of a product, reach and frequency (the distribution of ads and how often they should run), and creative considerations (such as the tone of the ad).

You'll spend considerable time using computers and spreadsheet programs, which speed up routine computation. You'll be analyzing research about the product and its customers or potential customers and extracting usable data from such numbers as the CPM (cost per thousand), the cost of reaching 1000 people in the target audience, and the GRP (gross rating points), the number of people reached for a certain expenditure.

Coming up with the right media mix is challenging because there are so many options. Although you'll know the budget the client has allocated for advertising, the media group may well recommend a higher or lower figure.

Once the client approves the media plan, buyers execute the decisions. In small agencies, planning and buying are often done by the same people, but in the larger ones the tasks are separate. Buyers are more marketing and sales-oriented, and negotiation is a big part of their job. Regional spot buyers, who buy air time on regional radio and television, usually aspire to be network spot buyers, because these buyers handle the most expensive advertising purchases of all.

QUALIFICATIONS

PERSONAL: Strong interpersonal skills. Ability to work as a member of a team. Good judgment. Willingness to assume responsibility for decisions.

PROFESSIONAL: Basic math skills. Ability to make oral presentations to groups. Strong writing skills.

CAREER PATHS

LEVEL	JOB TITLE	EXPERIENCE NEEDED
Entry	Assistant media planner	College degree
2	Media planner	3–5 years
3	Associate media director	5–7 years
4	Media director of planning	7–10 years
5	Media manager of planning and buying	10+ years

JOB RESPONSIBILITIES ♦ ENTRY LEVEL

THE BASICS: Learning to interpret rate cards of various media. Heavy computation. Doing work sheets. Analyzing audience ratings (such as Neilsen ratings). Writing letters and memos.

MORE CHALLENGING DUTIES: Comparing media alternatives. Preparing for and delivering presentations to clients. Talking to sales representatives from various media. Evaluating media buys.

MOVING UP

Although you must demonstrate basic competence with numbers, your promotability largely depends on selling your ideas about a particular campaign both to members of the team and, most important, to the client. Being able to handle pressure and crises will also help you land a place on interesting and challenging accounts. The most desirable ones are packaged-goods accounts, because these clients invest a lot of money in advertsing and demand quality service. After three years on packaged-goods accounts, you can often move into account services. Those who enjoy media planning stay on to become managers in that department if they demonstrate talent and administrative skills.

RESEARCH

The research department is the center of market analysis, consumer research, product evaluation, and concept testing—all the considerations that go into the formulation of a marketing strategy or an advertising campaign.

As an entry-level person, your main responsibilities will be to gather and organize data for the more experienced people in the department. You may be doing primary research, designing surveys to test a hypothesis about a particular product or the consumers who may buy it. In addition to deciding what kinds of questions should be asked and their format, you also pinpoint who the survey respondents should be and how they should be questioned. Once you've worked out all the details, you'll hand over the task of actually carrying out the survey to an outside "supplier," a market research firm. The supplier will present you with a summary of the research results, often rows and columns of numbers. Research analysts figure out what patterns and trends the numbers signify and how they should affect the marketing and advertising campaign.

Secondary research involves culling information published by the government, the trade, or other groups. You'll write reports summarizing the results, which may be used by the creative, account services, or media people.

Before an advertising campaign is created and implemented, the key issue researchers focus on is the consumer's perception of a particular product. Once the campaign is executed, the important thing to determine is whether the advertising is being correctly perceived by those for whom it is intended.

QUALIFICATIONS

PERSONAL: Problem-solving mentality. A logical, analytical mind. Ability to work independently, yet contribute to a team effort. Good organizational skills.

PROFESSIONAL: Good writing skills. Ability to work with statistics. Familiarity with data interpretation.

CAREER PATHS

LEVEL	JOB TITLE	EXPERIENCE NEEDED
Entry	Project director	College or graduate degree. One year of market research experience preferred.
2	Research account executive	1–3 years
3	Associate research director	3–8 years
4	Research director	7–10 years
5	Department manager	10+ years

JOB RESPONSIBILITIES ◆ ENTRY LEVEL

THE BASICS: Plenty of paperwork. Posting numbers from computer printouts. Researching printed literature.

MORE CHALLENGING DUTIES: Drafting reports from research. Getting competitive bids from suppliers. Sitting in on planning sessions. Suggesting new methods of data gathering. Helping design surveys.

MOVING UP

Demonstrating that you are a talented interpreter of the information you collect is critical in getting promoted, as is coming up with innovative ways to test product information, advertising strategy, or new markets. The more you are able to contribute to the success of a campaign, the more likely it is your star will rise quickly. If, on top of talents for research and analysis, you prove to be an adroit decision-maker, you can move into a management position. Research can also be a pathway to jobs in the account and media groups for those who are more business-oriented.

ACCOUNT SERVICES

Account executives serve as the link between the agency and the client. They oversee all aspects of an ad campaign, working with all other departments to make sure that problems are solved, that work is completed on time, and that everyone involved knows his or her responsibilities. The creative department looks to the account executive for information about the product and for help in creating campaign ideas. Those in research need direction to determine what information is needed about the product and its potential consumers. The media group works closely with the account executives to develop the best marketing strategy and media mix possible for the amount of money budgeted.

The client relies on the account executive to answer questions, correct misunderstandings, and take care of mistakes. Keeping a client happy can involve hand-holding, pacifying, reassuring, and being available for frequent consultations, while not neglecting other clients or the development of new prospects. Profitability is the bottom-line concern of account executives. Given that financial responsibility, two or more years of experience in the business is usually a prerequisite for a job, although some large agencies train particularly qualified candidates. If you were a business major in college and have worked as an intern or summer employee in product development for a major consumer goods manufacturer or in account services in an advertising agency, you may be considered for such a training program.

QUALIFICATIONS

PERSONAL: Good judgment. Strong interpersonal skills. Willingness to be on the firing line. Sensitivity to current trends. Leadership qualities.

PROFESSIONAL: Negotiation skills. Advertising or marketing experience. Knowledge of product development and manufacturing. Sales acumen.

CAREER PATHS

LEVEL	JOB TITLE	EXPERIENCE NEEDED
Entry	Account executive trainee	College degree. Advertising-related experience.
2	Account executive	1–3 years
3	Senior account executive	5–8 years
4	Accounts supervisor or manager	10–13 years

JOB RESPONSIBILITIES ◆ ENTRY LEVEL

THE BASICS: Fielding material from other departments. Taking calls from clients. Keeping in touch with the traffic department on schedules for ads and spots. Monitoring deadlines and pressing creative people for overdue copy. Following through on any marketing needs.

MORE CHALLENGING DUTIES: Meeting with clients. Participating in meetings with other departments. Consulting with the creative department on the ideas for a campaign. Planning an overall strategy for your client. Keeping up-to-date on media rate changes and new media outlets.

MOVING UP

Once you demonstrate that you're able to deal effectively with clients and work well with your colleagues in other departments, you'll be given a bigger role on a major account or possibly one or two small accounts of your own. (Even newcomers work on major accounts taking care of details for more senior account executives.) It is your responsibility to anticipate and prevent potential problems and confrontations while doing your best for both the agency and the client. Building a successful record of ad campaigns and developing a reputation for being easy to work with can eventually earn you the title of senior account executive.

Only those who are effective managers and have well-honed administrative skills eventually become account managers and supervisors, overseeing and nurturing a number of accounts and going after new business. They hold regular meetings with their sales group to point out prospects and build up a file of potential clients, and they engineer the agency pitch for new business.

ADDITIONAL INFORMATION

SALARIES

The trade magazine *Adweek* does an annual survey. The following figures, which represent the national median annual salary for each position, are taken from the most recent survey:

CREATIVE

Copywriter	$46,300
Creative director	$46,700

MEDIA

Media buyer	$26,100
Media planner	$26,100
Media department head	$37,300

RESEARCH

Research services director	$51,900

ACCOUNT SERVICES

Assistant account executive	$23,700
Account executive	$41,900
Account department head	$49,800

WORKING CONDITIONS

HOURS: Deadlines and emergencies are the normal course of business at most agencies. Clients must be satisfied, which often means putting in evening or weekend hours, depending on the pressure your department is under to produce.

ENVIRONMENT: Entry-level people in all departments often work in bullpens, but they generally share an office with one or two others. More experienced people have their own offices—and more privacy. Account people usually rate the most attractive office space because they meet with clients and are responsible for millions of dollars in billing.

WORKSTYLE: Creative, media, and account people spend a lot of time in meetings and presentations—with each other and with clients. When you're not discussing ideas and strategies, you'll be at your desk—working over copy if you're in creative or working with figures if you're in media. Account executives spend a lot of time on the phone with clients. Research staff spend their time designing surveys and working with outside market research firms. The media staff gets a coveted perk—lots of lunches paid for by the media sales representatives.

TRAVEL: Travel opportunities vary according to client needs, your position within the agency, and the size of the account, but, generally speaking, most work is done at the agency.

EXTRACURRICULAR ACTIVITIES/WORK EXPERIENCE

Campus newspaper or TV or radio station—writing, editing, space sales
Student-run business (or your own)—promoting, marketing, and selling a product or service
Market research firms—working as an intern or summer employee

INTERNSHIPS

The American Advertising Federation offers a variety of internship possibilities through its members nationwide. The scope of each program and the requirements vary from sponsor to sponsor. A complete list of members, which includes companies with in-house advertising departments and agencies, is available by writing to the American Advertising Federation. Interested students must inquire directly with sponsors, keeping in mind that not all members take interns.

RECOMMENDED READING

BOOKS
Advertising Career Directory, Ron Fry, ed., Career Press Inc.: 1987

Advertising Careers: How Advertising Works and the People Who Make It Happen by Jan Greenberg, Henry Holt & Company: 1987

Advertising: Concepts & Strategies by Harold W. Berkman and Christopher Gilson, 2nd ed., Random House: 1986

Guts: Advertising from the Inside Out by John Lyons, AMACOM: 1987

Blood, Brains, and Beer: An Autobiography by David Ogilvy, Antheneum Publishers: 1978

Breaking into Advertising: Making Your Portfolio Work for You by Ken Musto, Van Nos Reinhold: 1988

Confessions of an Advertising Man by David Ogilvy, Antheneum Publishers: 1980

How to Become an Advertising Man by James W. Young, National Textbook Company: 1987

How to Get Your First Copywriting Job in Advertising by Dick Wasserman, Dutton: 1987

Ogilvy on Advertising by David Ogilvy, Crown Publishers: 1979

So You Want to Be in Advertising: A Guide to Success in a Fast-Paced Business, Ed Caffrey, ed., Simon & Schuster: 1988

The Successful Advertiser: A Step-by-Step Guide to Managing Advertising in Today's Changing Marketplace by Stephen Baker, John Wiley and Sons: 1988

PERIODICALS

Advertising Age (weekly), Crain Communications, Inc., 740 North Rush Street, Chicago, IL 60611

Adweek (weekly), Adweek Publications, 820 Second Avenue, New York, NY 10017 (regional editions for East, Southeast, West, Southwest, and Midwest)

Folio (monthly), Hansen Publishing Group, 6 River Bend, Box 4949, Stamford, CT 06907

PROFESSIONAL ASSOCIATIONS

The Advertising Council
825 Third Avenue
New York, NY 10022

Advertising Research Foundation
Information Center
3 East 54th Street
New York, NY 10022

American Advertising Federation
1400 K Street, N.W.
Suite 1000
Washington, DC 20005

American Association of Advertising Agencies
666 Third Avenue
New York, NY 10017

Association of National Advertisers
155 East 44th Street
New York, NY 10017

INTERVIEWS

REES PINNEY
MEDIA BUYER/PLANNER
O'NEAL & PRELLE ADVERTISING AND PUBLIC RELATIONS
HARTFORD, CT

I found my job through the co-op department at the University of Hartford. Hartford had cooperative education which means you work for a company in the community, you get paid for it, and you get credits through the school. I majored in communications and English, participated in the co-op program, and O'Neal and Prelle hired me full time after I graduated.

We are a full service ad agency. We get clients and they tell us what kind of products they have. We develop a creative message for them. They give us a budget and they tell us who they want to reach, or what kind of target audience they want. My job is to figure out where they should advertise to reach their target audience within their budget restraints. For example, if they want to reach males between the ages of 18 to 49, and they've got $100,000 to spend, I might put them into a very heavy radio schedule with some sports television thrown in for good measure. These are all kind of clichés, but if you wanted to reach women you'd place the ad on soap operas. You would also want to hit consumer magazines like regional editions of *People Magazine* or *Better Homes and Garden*. So I devise the media plan and then I execute it.

A typical day for me includes buying the time or the space for advertments. I also monitor the commercials and advertisements. A big part of the process is to meet with advertising reps. This is important because I am a buyer and all the sales representatives for the outlets, either broadcast stations or magazines, want to sell me their product—which is either space or time. So I spend a lot of time listening to pitches and trying to determine if this is indeed the right vehicle for my clients.

The best thing to do to break into advertising, and I may be biased in that this is the way I did it, is to get involved with the field while you are still in school. Most schools have excellent connections with the community and can get you, if not a co-op paid position, an internship. More often than not, these departments at colleges are under-utilized. Now, if you don't go through your college, the next best thing is to just pound the pavement. Get to know people and target your résumé to the specific job you want in advertising. Advertising is a rather large field—you can do creative, you can do account work, there is media work, which is what I do, and then there is production, etc. If you have an arts background, get together a portfolio and get in touch with creative directors. If you really enjoy working with people then you should pursue the account side of the business. Call up the president, tell him that you are a people person and that you want to work with clients. Get yourself into the office.

If you want to move up in the field you've got to work very hard. Always know what is expected of you and then try to do a little bit more. Go that extra mile—stay late, get there early, take on added responsibilities. I know these sound like clichés but in this business, at least, they work. If you are there for people that's going to show. If you don't get credit, call attention to yourself. Don't be arrogant, ask how you can improve on what you are doing and that will bring to your boss's attention that you are in fact doing things.

A person in advertising has to be aggressive. You can't be intimidated. In the creative department you are kind of insulated, but in the other areas of advertising you are out there with people all the time. You can't be afraid to call someone on the phone and let them know that you aren't happy about where they ran your spot. If you buy a rotation in prime time and it runs somewhere else, you've got to be able to call the station and demand that they put the commercial where you want it. No one does these things for you, you've got to have the initiative. You've got to be thorough and accurate.

I like meeting a lot of people. I mean the ad biz is a really social biz. You go out to a lot of socials and mixers, which can grow tedious, but you come into contact with a lot of interesting and powerful people. Big clients have big dollars and its fun to have some control over what they do with their resources. I like the satisfaction of seeing my work bear some fruit. When I am watching a television show and one of my commercials comes on, it's not exciting for anyone else, but I can say "Hey, I put that there" and that's satisfying.

Since I am somewhat down the corporate ladder I have some work that can only be described as drudgery. I am responsible for billing. The buying process itself, after you've devised the plan, is a lot of paperwork. You've got to put data on the computer, mail out tape to television stations, print out reports, etc. I don't really enjoy that aspect of my work, but as long as it's kept under control and the weight is balanced on the shoulders of other workers, I don't get too upset about it. I realize that no job is perfect (unless you are announcing baseball games).

I would advise people who are interested in advertising to not waste their college years. Go out there and start laying the groundwork for your career, which is your future. Even if you know that you aren't going straight into advertising—say you are going to travel in Europe and then go to graduate school—it doesn't hurt to get known in the community where you went to school or your home community. Work summers in the ad business, or get an internship. But get started early because there is a lot of competition to get into the business.

AL PAUL LEFTON, JR.
PRESIDENT, CHIEF EXECUTIVE OFFICER
AL PAUL LEFTON COMPANY, INC.
PHILADELPHIA, PA

I started in advertising in 1950 after graduating from Yale. Yale had a divisional major called Sociology, History, and Literature, which I found to be very helpful, especially the sociology courses.

I interview starting-level people. Good grades and the ability to write well and express oneself clearly are essential. The particular academic major is not especially important, but it has to have something to do with words—journalism, English literature, liberal arts.

I would recommend that you do something to make your application different from all the others. I get hundreds of résumés that all look the same. Of course, if the pages are stapled out of order, if postage is due or if the cover letter has misspellings (I get a lot where my name is misspelled!), they go right into the wastebasket.

I am not impressed by gratuitous compliments about our agency that I know are being made about every other agency. I look for applications that show that the writer has done some research, perhaps about a new account we have or that offer some pertinent and interesting observation about a current one.

In the interview, I look for a very high degree of interpersonal skills, fair-mindedness, and balance, for someone who is a good strategist and has a sense of drama and attention to details.

Entry-level positions in advertising often involve a lot of clerical work. The next step on the business side is to an assistant's post, quite often in media or account service. This type of job involves a lot of paperwork and very little decision-making, but it provides the opportunity to learn from firsthand experience. At the next step, account executive, you begin to have some autonomy. It is at this level that you either sink or swim. You have the responsibility for properly servicing an account and making it grow. If you prove to be competent and skillful, you advance to the next level, account supervisor, and beyond that to management supervisor.

Is there security in the agency business? Well, it clearly does not provide the security of a government job. But for all the challenges and diversity of assignments, there have to be risks.

Our industry has gone through remarkable increases in productivity. Twenty years ago, it used to take nine people to handle a million dollars in billings. It now takes only three people per million dollars, and that figure will decline further with increased use of computers, which we now use heavily in testing media schedules and doing in-house typography. Like most fields, advertising has its highs and lows. During those periods when you have to get ready for a sales meeting or put together a presentation which is crucial to the growth of new business, you simply have to postpone your social life. What I like most about advertising is that you don't do the same thing on any given day. There is always a different kind of client problem to solve.

BANKING

I t wasn't too long ago that people who seemed to have easy jobs that didn't take up too much of their time were said to have "banker's hours." The analogy goes back to the days when bank business was conducted from nine in the morning to three in the afternoon, five days a week. No more, no less.

Those days are long gone. The banking industry is a fiercely competitive, round-the-clock arena that is the focal point of the national and world economy. Deregulation of the industry has opened the floodgates to a rush of services that banks now provide their customers. It has also made the banking business much more complex and greatly accelerated the need for the kinds of skills an M.B.A. holder has to offer.

The banking business has a well-deserved reputation for being rock-steady, but developments in the 1980's point up the fact that heightened competitive pressures can cause even the steadiest of industries to falter. On the national level, hundreds of small banks—primarily savings and loan institutions—failed in the 1980s, primarily due to drastic economic downturns in the Southwest. Investigations revealed that many banks that failed had engaged in unwise, improper, and in some cases, illegal financial dealings. It is estimated that the federal government will spend billions of dollars to bail out such troubled institutions—and it's certain that this aid will carry with it tighter restrictions on how banks operate.

In the international arena, large banks are dealing with a financial crisis of their own. For years, banks have advanced loans to foreign nations, particularly developing nations with significant natural resources, to help those nations build their economies. For nations that counted on energy resources for revenue, such as Mexico with its huge oil reserves, the rapid decline of energy prices in the 1980's proved catastrophic. As a result, borrower nations in many cases can't—and in some cases won't—pay the interest that continues to pile up on their loans. Lending banks are having some success in arranging for some sort of less onerous payment schemes on the part of debtor nations, but it's clear that the oil bust of the 1980's will have a significant impact on how banks deal with governments in the coming years.

As a result of the uncertainty and rapidly changing market conditions, banks in some cases have decided that the best way to weather the storm is to join forces. Many larger banks, including regional commercial banks, have embarked on an aggressive merger and acquisition path in the past few years. As some of these regional banks grow larger, the prospects for even greater competition on the national scene are also growing.

Many of the changes in banking are due to the impact of technology. Automated teller machines, global electronic funds transfer systems, and office automation in general have affected every bank employee. But you don't have to be a whiz kid who talks in bits and bytes to get your foot in the door. Every major bank has either a formal training program or professional on-the-job training that includes instruction in the use of the technology. What is most important is your ability to grasp the concepts and quickly master the skills.

More and more students entering the field have had the foresight to make themselves knowledgeable about telecommunications in order to gain an understanding of the newly diverse world of banking. These students have a better chance of getting a job offer than those with a limited, traditional view of the industry.

The industry welcomes M.B.A. graduates from a wide variety of backgrounds. Graduate concentrations in finance, marketing, and accounting are often preferred, but any M.B.A. concentration is acceptable. Your undergraduate major is of less concern to employers. A candidate with a liberal arts background may enter the industry as easily as one with an undergraduate degree in a business-related discipline.

Most banks put all new employees through a training program. Some M.B.A.s, depending on their backgrounds and their employers' policies, will not be placed in a formal training program, but will receive their orientation on the job. Simply having an M.B.A. will not spare you from performing routine entry-level duties, but you can expect to gain responsibility and receive your first promotion much more quickly than non-M.B.A., entry-level employees.

Commercial banking recruits M.B.A.s chiefly for the following functional areas:

♦ **CREDIT LENDING**

♦ **OPERATIONS/FINANCIAL SERVICES**

♦ **SYSTEMS**

♦ **TRUSTS**

JOB OUTLOOK

JOB OPENINGS WILL GROW: Faster than average

COMPETITION FOR JOBS: Keen

Expect the most competition for positions in credit lending. Expanding opportunities can be found in the operations/financial services and systems areas. As new sources for loans become harder to find, operations is being looked to for development of fee-based services, such as letters of credit and money transfer services. In systems, the computerization and communications systems needed to deliver customer services are implemented.

NEW JOB OPPORTUNITIES: Because of industry deregulation, banks are now actively seeking people to work in such diverse areas as mergers and acquisitions, private banking (which serves individuals with high net worth and high incomes), office automation (which develops executive information systems and implements them throughout the bank), product management (which includes the planning, pricing, and marketing of new products and services) and telecommunications (which develops the global communications channels necessary for getting and submitting information).

The skills of the M.B.A. are specifically needed in specialized areas, such as international banking and multinational corporate accounts, that require exceptional analytical skills and the ability to handle unusually large and complex problems.

GEOGRAPHIC JOB INDEX

Although banks can be found in any city or town, the major money centers are located in New York, NY, Chicago, IL, San Francisco, CA, and Boston, MA.

WHO THE EMPLOYERS ARE

COMMERCIAL BANKS (or money-center banks) market their products and services to multinational corporations, smaller banks (called correspondents), and individuals (who use checking and loan services).

REGIONAL BANKS provide many of the same services as the larger money-center banks, but on a smaller scale. Their clients are typically locally based small- and medium-size businesses.

SAVINGS AND LOAN ASSOCIATIONS offer their customers personal savings accounts and mortgages. They are also allowed to make commercial and business loans.

MAJOR EMPLOYERS

MULTINATIONAL COMMERCIAL BANKS
BankAmerica Corp., San Francisco, CA
Bankers Trust New York Corp., New York, NY
Bank of Boston Corp., Boston, MA
The Chase Manhattan Corp., New York, NY
Chemical Banking Corp., New York, NY
Citicorp, New York, NY
Continental Bank Corp., Chicago, IL
First Chicago Corp., Chicago, IL
Irving Bank Corp., New York, NY
J. P. Morgan & Co., Inc., New York, NY

REGIONAL COMMERCIAL BANKS
Bancorp Hawaii, Inc., Honolulu, HI
CoreStates Financial Corp., Philadelphia, PA
First of America Bank Corp., Kalamazoo, MI
First Union Corp., Charlotte, NC
First Wachovia Corp., Winston-Salem, NC
Fleet/Norstar Financial Group, Inc., Providence, RI
Old Kent Financial Corp., Grand Rapids, MI
Premier Bancorp, Inc., Baton Rouge, LA
Sovran Financial Corp., Norfolk, VA
State Street Boston Corp., Boston, MA

HOW TO BREAK INTO THE FIELD

Do not wait until after you have your M.B.A. to investigate banking. Many banks are eager to have business school students participate in summer internships. This experience is required by a few employers and preferred by most. If you choose to become a full-time employee at the bank and in the department in which you were an intern, you may move more quickly through training or bypass it completely.

Before any interview—whether it is for an internship or a full-time job—do your homework. Learn all you can about the internal workings of the area in which you plan to interview. If your field of interest is not represented, select the next most appropriate area and ask the recruiter to forward your résumé to the proper section. Also learn something about the bank itself. Different banks have different personalities. Some are aggressive, others more traditional and conservative. Try to interview with banks whose corporate identity is compatible with your own.

INTERNATIONAL JOB OPPORTUNITIES

The chance to work overseas does exist in banks with international operations. If you are interested in working abroad, you should apply to work in the international department. There you may have the opportunity to alternate assignments of perhaps three to five years abroad with stints in the United States. Competence in a foreign language is helpful but not a requirement because your employer will provide language instruction.

With international experience you might eventually become involved in financial consulting, working with corporations and governments. With international debts soaring, international banking has become a challenging, dynamic area that needs the best and the brightest.

CREDIT LENDING

This is the most visible area of banking and includes the traditional bank-client relationship that almost everyone associates with the industry. However, there is more to this aspect of banking than just extending credit or offering interest-bearing accounts to clients. In consumer banking, a lending officer assesses the creditworthiness of individuals. In commercial banking, officers evaluate the financial status of corporations or nonprofit organizations; perform industry surveys, analyzing a particular industry to determine if backing a firm in that area is a good loan risk; make production forecasts to see if a borrowing firm's available resources will meet production requirements; predict how a loan would affect positively or negatively the bank's cash flow; or handle corporate overdrafts, contacting corporate customers whose payments are not on time.

During training you will go on customer calls with experienced loan officers and be responsible for taking notes and writing a report on the customer and the loan review, not as a participant but as an observer. You may be called on to research new business prospects, making cold calls to prospects in a given territory or industry. Your responsibilities will soon grow broader, and you will begin making decisions on modest loans.

QUALIFICATIONS

PERSONAL: Strong analytical skills. Ability to conceptualize. An affinity for quantitative problems. Strong negotiation skills. Extremely good interpersonal skills.

PROFESSIONAL: Ability to analyze data and financial statements and do creative financial planning. Familiarity with bank products and services. Ability to present clearly written reports.

CAREER PATHS

LEVEL	JOB TITLE	EXPERIENCE NEEDED
Entry	Trainee	Internship experience often preferred
2	Assistant loan officer	6 months–1 year
3	Loan officer/branch manager	2–4 years
4	Loan manager	5+ years

JOB RESPONSIBILITIES ♦ ENTRY LEVEL

THE BASICS: Training will consist of both classroom instruction in finance, accounting, credit analysis, and so forth, and actual account work, helping lending officers make judgments about existing or potential bank relationships.

MORE CHALLENGING DUTIES: Upon completion of training, you will be assigned to a line lending area, attend advanced banking seminars, and have the opportunity to meet with customers.

MOVING UP

Your advancement will depend on your ability to establish advantageous client relationships, the successful closing of lucrative loan deals, and knowing when not to approve a loan. As you advance, the loan review process will become more complex and involve significantly more money. You can measure your success by your approval authority—how big a loan you are authorized to approve without going to a higher level of management.

OPERATIONS/FINANCIAL SERVICES

Few banks today are in the business solely of safeguarding money and loaning it to creditworthy businesses and individuals. All major banks and many smaller ones offer their customers a full range of financial services. These services, for which banks collect fees, range from providing letters of credit, money transfers, and foreign exchanges services to offering credit cards and financial planning services.

Such services typically are grouped under the heading "operations." In the case of larger banks, such services have expanded to the extent that the banks have set up separate subsidiary companies to provide the services, to the point that bank operations departments seem to have disappeared. Whether you call it an operations department or a subsidiary service, the financial services segment has become a critical component of the banking industry.

As with other areas in the banking business, a career in operations requires a period of training. The length of your training depends on how much exposure you have had to bank operations. You will move into a supervisory position, managing the clerical staff, with responsibility for setting up assignments and time schedules, evaluating performance, making sure work is done properly, training new employees, authorizing salary increases. Work in operations also involves troubleshooting for customers; for example, solving an account problem by tracing a money transfer that was never credited.

QUALIFICATIONS

PERSONAL: Ability to meet deadlines. Ability to perform under pressure. Ability to get along with many different types of people.

PROFESSIONAL: Ability to understand and follow through on complex instructions. Familiarity with concepts of computer science or a related discipline. Knowledge of fee-based services and products.

CAREER PATHS

LEVEL	JOB TITLE	EXPERIENCE NEEDED
Entry	Operations	Prior experience often preferred
2	Supervisor	Up to 1 year
3	Department manager	2–3 years
4	Division manager	5 + years

JOB RESPONSIBILITIES ♦ ENTRY LEVEL

THE BASICS: You begin your career in operations either in a formal training program, or, more likely, on the job. You will be an operations trainee for about 18 months, learning by rotating among the various departments that handle fee-based services.

MORE CHALLENGING DUTIES: After the training period, you will be assigned to a department or a staff area such as financial management or budget coordination and will learn about a single product or area in depth.

MOVING UP

Your progress will depend on your ability to improve the overall productivity of your department or area, to motivate your staff, to stay within your budget, and to complete transactions efficiently and accurately. Because operations is not exclusively devoted to production management, for further advancement you will need to learn about product development, marketing, and systems functions. Those who move into these areas often accompany loan officers on customer calls, offering the technical advice that will help clinch a deal, or presenting a plan to customize an existing product to meet the expanding needs of the client.

With hard work and diligence you can acquire the knowledge and expertise that will enable you to move almost anywhere in the bank organization. Operations managers can move into marketing positions, the systems areas, or perhaps relocate (even overseas) to manage a branch office.

SYSTEMS

The systems area is now involved in every banking decision from credit lending to recruitment. Most large commercial banks have both a central systems area and separate decentralized systems units that service the major components of the organization. Systems is responsible for developing, implementing, and maintaining automated programs for clients and in-house use, for selecting hardware, writing software, and consulting with the user/client when there is a need to develop special programs. In addition, systems staffers must keep up with the latest developments in technological applications and services.

QUALIFICATIONS

PERSONAL: Ability to think in analytical terms. Ease in working with abstract models.

PROFESSIONAL: Quantitative skills. Familiarity with the business applications of software and hardware. Ability to convert technical language and concepts into familiar and understandable terms.

CAREER PATHS

LEVEL	JOB TITLE	EXPERIENCE NEEDED
Entry	Systems trainee	Prior experience in banking or business computing often preferred
2	Systems analyst	1 year
3	Systems consultant	2–3 years
4	Senior systems consultant	4–5 years

JOB RESPONSIBILITIES ♦ ENTRY LEVEL

THE BASICS: In either a structured training program or through on-the-job training, you will become familiar with the bank's hardware and software and how they are used. You will be placed on a systems team project, refining the use of current equipment or developing systems for as yet unmet needs.

MORE CHALLENGING DUTIES: Applying your skills to more difficult or specialized projects.

MOVING UP

If you demonstrate interpersonal skills as well as technical ability, you could become a project manager, overseeing a team of systems people working on the development and implementation of a specific systems capability, such as a new internal telephone switching system, or software for an executive workstation, which could include features such as electronic mail and word processing.

The potential for a talented systems person is excellent. You could end up managing an operations or office automation department, developing and intalling new systems, or becoming a systems consultant for overseas branches. Successful systems personnel can move into any department in the bank.

TRUSTS

The trust department manages and invests money, property or other assets owned by a client. The pension plans of large corporations and other organizations often use trusts, as do individuals with large assets. Many estates, by the provisions of a will, are also managed in trust. This department, like the credit department, deals closely and extensively with clients. The training program is similar to that in other areas of banking, but in general advancement is slower and requires more experience.

QUALIFICATIONS

PERSONAL: A straightforward manner. Accuracy. Good with numbers. Patience in dealing with people. Confidence.

PROFESSIONAL: Strong analytical ability. Good business judgment. Ability to apply financial theory to practical problems.

CAREER PATHS

LEVEL	JOB TITLE	EXPERIENCE NEEDED
Entry	Trainee	Banking experience often preferred
2	Assistant trust officer	1–2 years
3	Trust officer	3–6 years
4	Senior trust officer	10+ years

JOB RESPONSIBILITIES ♦ ENTRY LEVEL

THE BASICS: Developing a familiarity with bank policies and procedures.

MORE CHALLENGING DUTIES: Researching investments, real estate, or the overall economy in order to assist superiors. Some contact with clients.

MOVING UP

Showing sound judgment and an ability to work independently will garner an assignment to manage some of the smaller trust funds. Moving up also depends on your ability to attract new customers to the bank, as well as to keep present clients satisfied. As you advance you will become responsible for handling more and more money. Top level trust officers are expected not only to bring in substantial new business and to handle the largest accounts, but also to manage and support lower level employees.

ADDITIONAL INFORMATION

SALARIES

Annual salaries vary according to the size of the bank. The following figures are taken from Robert Half International's most recent survey:

Trust Staff (Corporate/Personal): $19,000 to $27,500 (medium/small banks—less than $300 million in assets); $18,000 to $27,000 (large—$300 million and higher).

Trust Officer (Corporate/Personal): $26,000 to $36,000 (medium/small); $33,000 to $43,000 (large).

Loan or Operations Staff (Domestic/International): $16,000 to $24,000 (medium/small); $18,500 to $25,500 (large).

Loan or Operations Supervisor (Assistant Branch Manager—Domestic/International): $19,000 to $25,000 (medium/small); $19,000 to $27,000 (large).

Operations Officer/Branch Manager (Domestic/International): $23,000 to $35,000 (medium/small); $29,500 to $37,500 (large).

Credit Analyst: $21,000 to $27,000 (medium/small); $23,500 to $28,500 (large).

Mortgage Lenders (Commercial, Residential): $27,500 to $42,000 (medium/small); $38,000 to $49,000 (large).

Consumer Lenders: $22,000 to $32,000 (medium/small); $27,500 to $34,000 (large).

Commercial Lenders (3+ years experience): $32,000 to $42,000 (medium/small, corporate, middle market); $35,000 to $45,000 (large, corporate, middle market).

Commercial Lenders (1–3 years experience): $21,000 to $27,000 (medium/small, corporate, middle market); $23,000 to $32,000 (large, corporate, middle market).

Senior Loan Officer: $36,000 to $47,000 (medium/small); $40,000 to $59,000 (large).

WORKING CONDITIONS

HOURS: The credit trainee rarely sees daylight, because long hours and weekend work are often required to get through the training program. After training, normal hours will be whatever it takes to get the job done (nine-to-five plus). The hours in operations are different because it is a 24-hour-a-day shop. Night shifts and weekend work may be unavoidable, especially for less experienced employees. Systems staffers may also work on a 24-hour clock; the hours are longest when new systems are being installed and deadlines must be met.

ENVIRONMENT: Lending officers get the choicest locations in the bank; because their job is customer-oriented, the surroundings are usually plush and pleasant. The operations and systems departments take a 360-degree turn from the lending department; the workspace is strictly functional, with few amenities.

WORKSTYLE: In credit, much time is spent researching facts and figures about existing and prospective clients, which could take you from the bank library to the client's headquarters. The rest of your time will largely be spent in conference with senior lending officers. Operations and systems work is desk work. Managers walk the area, talking with the staff and lending assistance. In both of these departments, senior people may meet occasionally with systems consultants.

TRAVEL: Travel is rare for entry-level employees in any bank. Later, however, lending officers in consumer banking might travel throughout their state. In commercial banking, research could take a lending officer to major cities throughout the country. If you are assigned to the international department in credit, operations, or systems, you might be sent to overseas branches.

INTERNSHIPS

Ample internship opportunities are available for the M.B.A. who is interested in a banking career. You should investigate internship openings—both the department in which you intern and the bank for which you work—as carefully as you would look for a full-time job. Many banks recruit on campus for interns, but you should also make inquiries on your own to those that do not.

RECOMMENDED READING

BOOKS

Banking Strategies for Business: A Guide for the Independent Manager by Bryan E. Milling, Chilton Books: 1987

Excellence in Banking by Steven I. Davis, St. Martin's Press: 1985

Money, Banking, and Economic Analysis, 3rd ed., by Thomas D. Simpson, Prentice-Hall: 1987

Money, Financial Institutions, and Economic Activity by Bruce R. Dalgaard, Scott, Foresman: 1987

Polk's Bank Directory, Int'l. Edition, R. L. Polk and Company: updated regularly.

PERIODICALS

ABA Banking Journal (monthly), 345 Hudson Street, New York, NY 10014

American Banker (daily), One State Street Plaza, New York, NY 10004

The Banker's Magazine (bimonthly), Warren, Gorham, and Lamont, Inc., One Penn Plaza, New York, NY 10119

Bank News (monthly), 912 Baltimore Avenue, Kansas City, MO 64105

PROFESSIONAL ASSOCIATIONS

American Bankers Association
1120 Connecticut Avenue, N.W.
Washington, DC 20036

Consumer Bankers Association
1300 North 17th Street
Arlington, VA 22209

National Association of Bank Women
500 North Michigan Avenue
Chicago, IL 60611

United States League of Savings Institutions
111 East Wacker Drive
Chicago, IL 60601

INTERVIEWS

VICE PRESIDENT
MAJOR COMMERCIAL BANK

I went to Iowa State University and majored in distributed studies, a curriculum I arranged with three areas of concentration; industrial administration, economics, and industrial engineering. My engineering studies emphasized capital budgeting and financial project management. When I graduated I looked for a job, and got tired of people asking me if I could type—which I couldn't. While I was in college I had spent some time in Japan doing a research project on the role of women in Japanese business, and I had become quite intrigued with the country. After four or five months of looking, when I really couldn't find the kind of job that I thought I should have, I made some contacts with people I had met in Japan and got a job teaching English, and picked up and went back. I stayed there for about a year and a half, and during that time I ended up working for a couple of small trading companies doing mostly English correspondence. I had a lot of time to talk to the people and find out what their business was like. I was always interested in business, and I had every intention of eventually going and getting an M.B.A. I knew I didn't want to do it right out of college, because what do you have to contribute, except what you learned in a book?

While I was overseas I did all my applications for business schools, and I came back to go directly to Harvard. When I was looking for a business school I knew that, having a technical undergraduate background, I wanted something a little less technical with more emphasis on communications. By the time I got to Harvard I knew I was interested in international business. I probably would not have chosen that coming right out of undergraduate school. I also knew that finance was my strongest suit, and I tailored my curriculum to that.

During the summer between my first and second year, I went to work for my employer as an intern in their European division, primarily to see if I liked international banking. It's an easy way to test a new career and one I'd recommend for everybody. During my second year I interviewed exclusively with banks because I wanted to go back overseas as rapidly as possible. I felt that banking was probably the easier way to do that. In hindsight though, I think it would have been better to have a wider choice of options and then narrow the field. In the end I went back to my former bank because I liked the atmosphere, but I also felt that, having worked in the European division over the summer, I could probably get an overseas assignment relatively quickly. As it turned out that was not the case due to a worldwide reorganization and the creation of the bank's multinational banking department. With all the moving around of people, Europe was pretty much closed off; at that time only our branches there were large enough to take people who didn't have too much experience. The way the Asia group was run you typically had to spend a couple of years at headquarters before you went overseas. So that's what I did. I spent two years being the liaison primarily to Taiwan, but also for Hong Kong and Korea, and then was transferred to Taipei.

In Taiwan for the first two years I was an account officer. Most M.B.A.s coming out of school and joining the lending side of a major bank would be account officers. An officer is assigned anywhere from ten to forty accounts, depending on the size of the accounts and the kind of business you do. At our bank, an account officer has responsibility for marketing, credit recommendations, and credit structuring. So on any given day you may go out and make several calls on your customers or on prospects to become acquainted with the kinds of business they do, and to see what kinds of services—be it money lending, cash management, or trust business—you can sell them. In Taiwan that meant mostly trade finance, letters of credit, and other documentary business, that is, processing documents for imports and exports. Like most countries, Taiwan has relatively complicated investment and financing laws and regulations and it was important to understand those fully in order to be able to advise customers. In fact, I think one of my more important roles was to act as a consultant to foreign companies doing business in Taiwan as to how best to structure and finance their companies—satisfying their own requirements yet staying with the local regulations.

I came back to the States about a year ago to be part of a newly created division which does an independent review and evaluation of all the risk assets of the bank. We look at every loan that is done within the bank and assign it a risk rating, based on the financial condition of the company, the industry, and so forth. We do both international and domestic transactions, but I've been working only on the domestic side. I cover about ten industry groupings, including cable television, forest products, and construction engineering.

There are a couple of things I really like about my present job. Because I have had a totally international background, being involved in domestic business is very interesting. The lending practices in the United States are in general much more sophisticated than they are in Taiwan. There are a lot of interesting financing structures that I've learned about in the last year, as well as legal aspects I'd never dealt with before. Also, being essentially an industry analyst is very challenging. That means looking in depth first of all at what we do: Are we comfortable with the level of risk we've got in a given industry? Why are we? I look at the characteristics of the industry, the companies, and the kinds of projects we lend to. It means delving into the industry itself. With this kind of job it's possible to act as a clearinghouse and a provider of information, which is a role I enjoy.

There's an opportunity to do a lot of facilitating in a field like banking. Most banks are structured so that you can be a generalist or you can become an industry specialist. Even as a generalist you get to know certain industries well. For example, in Taiwan I ended up doing a lot of lending to the petrochemical industry, and became a source for people in Asia. It's important to use your knowledge and experience to develop unique skills—which can be used in the bank or on the outside, for that matter.

JOHN TOMES
BANKING ASSOCIATE
CONTINENTAL BANK N.A.
LOS ANGELES, CA

I was a pre-med student at Kenyon College in Ohio. During the summers, I worked on offshore oil-rigs in the Gulf of Mexico, the Pacific, and the North Sea, which I think gave me a sense of the value of education and made me eager to complete my studies. However, although I'd been accepted to medical school during my last year, I decided instead to pursue my interest in business. I took a job with a medical consulting firm as an analyst, helping hospital groups make purchase decisions for equipment like nuclear magnetic resonance machines.

There were many analysts with M.B.A.s at this consultancy, and soon I saw that although I was competent without the degree, it would add considerably to my technical ability to go for that degree, and I signed up for a program at the University of Chicago.

As graduation drew near, I entered a summer internship at Continental Bank. I interviewed with investment banks as well as commercial banks like Continental. At one point in time, the distinction between the two was considerable, but with banks like Continental, the boundaries defining our respective roles are disappearing. Now much of our competition at Continental comes from investment banks instead of other commerical banks.

Continental is exclusively a business bank. Its funding is not predominantly derived from retail channels, as is that of many commercial banks. Instead, we are funded from Eurodollar, federal funds, repos, floating-rate term funds, and money market sources. The bank's clients are businesses seeking risk management advice, acquisition and restructuring financing, and money lending.

Banking today involves advising corporations about their financial activities, such as whether a proposed acquisition is really a good idea, or whether to divest a particular business and start another. Sometimes businesses become overly fond of the industry or business they started out in, although it may no longer be in their best interest to continue in that vein. Our job at Continental is to counsel companies about issues like that, as well as to provide expert financial advice and services.

Sometimes one of the most challenging aspects of this job is learning how to work with people within the bank, convincing them to take the risk of lending money to a client. While banks like Continental have substantial financial muscle, it is still a great risk to lend money. If a loan goes sour, it takes a long time to earn enough interest income to absorb the principal lost. So officers are careful, and part of my work is doing the financial modeling and analyses that will help them feel secure in lending support to a particular project, as well as understanding the risks associated with the transaction. Risk management involves protecting assets and cash flows against interest rate and foreign exchange risk. Products such as interest rate swaps and collars are part of managing risk.

Once the bank makes a commitment to loan money, other challenges emerge. For larger sums, over $200 million, for example, we generally call other banks to participate in a banking group. This lowers the risk for any individual lender by reducing the banks' exposure to one individual deal. At this point, there is frequently more negotiating and figuring.

A typical day may start with calling on a client with whom we've established a relationship. My boss, who is a vice president, will lead the conversation. I contribute as needed to her remarks with information I've gathered during the preceding week, day, or evening. Generally, we will meet with the chief financial officer of the client company, or in the case of smaller firms, with the chairman of the board or the president, and his chief financial officer.

Usually, we make about fifteen to twenty of these calls a month, and there is considerable travel within California. My boss and I are responsbile, among other accounts, for the Los Angeles entertainment industry businesses, so there are exciting opportunities to meet top-level executives of motion picture and production companies, and even to attend screenings of new movies. I've had to learn a great deal about that business, about what adds value for companies in the entertainment industry.

Banking is a lot of fun, but there is quite a personal commitment involved too. Days are frequently long, and if a deal is pending it's imperative to stay until the job is finished. That frequently means staying the weekend. But the rewards are there with a bank like Continental, and I enjoy my job and feel challenged by it. You can't "fake it" in this business. You find yourself frequently confronted by senior managers and company officers demanding your financial insights, and if you're not competent, it will show up pretty fast.

DEPARTMENT STORE RETAILING

Consumers generally take for granted that they will always find their favorite department stores brimming with merchandise. Unnoticed by most customers, a large, talented staff works long, hard hours to keep the shelves filled, the selection varied, the stores beautiful, and the business of retailing running smoothly. Retailing is an industry in which brains and diligence can take you to high levels of decision-making years before your contemporaries in other fields have reached similar positions of responsibility.

Graduates of virtually any discipline may enter department store retailing. Prospective employers are looking for demonstrated capacity to learn and make quick, sound judgments and are less interested in academic backgrounds. You must be flexible, comfortable with people, self-disciplined, and highly motivated—and a sense of humor certainly does not hurt. Retailing is a high-pressure profession where no slow seasons exist—only busy and busier, with the November-December pre-Christmas rush being the most hectic time of all. Prior retail experience, even a summer spent behind a cash register, is a plus; some retailers won't consider candidates without it.

Department store chains, once noted for their consistency and stability, have been caught up in the whirlwind of corporate mergers and takeovers that has been sweeping across the American business landscape since the mid-1980's. Many of the most recognizable names in the business—B. Altman, Bloomingdales, Bonwit Teller, and A&S, among others—have changed ownership at least once, as retail-chain conglomerates like Federated Department Stores and Allied Stores shuffle and reshuffle their holdings. No less a pillar of business than Sears, Roebuck, a fixture in American society since the dawn of the 20th century, has remolded itself to keep pace with its competition.

A big reason for this instability, of course, is the rise of the shopping mall. Multiple-store malls are now ubiquitous in most areas of the country. For the most part, these malls consist of one or two large department stores and a host of smaller specialty shops and boutiques. The competition from smaller shops has become increasingly intense. Although smaller stores can't match the big chains when it comes to variety and price, by specializing they can lure customers away. For this reason, many chains have abandoned the practice of offering steady but predictable merchandise in favor of infusing more creativity into the sales process. To do this, they need creative people who have a good idea about what customers want and how to present it.

Most entry-level jobs are in merchandising, an area further divided into:

◆ Store Management

◆ Buying

The talents of the art major are specifically in demand in two small, specialized job areas:

◆ Fashion Coordination

◆ Display

Fashion coordination is a job area found only in larger stores; neither job area employs a large staff, but both areas require a strong creative flair.

Most entry-level jobs are in merchandising. Your job in merchandising begins with a training period of six months to a year. Some trainees divide their time between classroom learning and work experience, others train entirely on the job. Generally, the larger the retailer, the more formalized the training. Whether you enter the field via store management or buying depends primarily on the employer. Many stores separate these functions beginning at the entry level. You must choose which path you prefer. Other stores will introduce all new merchandising personnel to buying and later allow those interested in and qualified for management to move up. The opposite arrangement, moving into buying at some later stage, also occurs, although infrequently.

The modern store is reaping the benefits of the technological revolution. Point-of-sale computer terminals are replacing mechanical cash registers. These automatically compute sales, taxes, and discounts and simplify inventory control by keeping sales records. Computers are also used for credit records and tracking sales forecasts.

Retailing is vulnerable to downturns in the economy, but it's one of the first industries to bounce back after a recession. As a highly profit-oriented business, it's hectic and competitive. The customer's satisfaction and loyalty to the store are very important, which means that you must tolerate and even pamper people whom you may not like. In retailing, the unexpected is the order of the day. You can expect to feel pressured, but seldom unchallenged.

JOB OUTLOOK

JOB OPENINGS WILL GROW: As fast as average

COMPETITION FOR JOBS: Keen. In merchandising, the most competition exists in buying; this area has fewer openings, tends to pay a bit better and has an aura of glamour about it.

NEW JOB OPPORTUNITIES: Most department store chains have retrenched over the past few years. The days when department stores sold everything from appliances to zippers are pretty much gone. Most chains now focus their attention on items that provide them with the highest markup (price above cost) and lowest inventory costs. Clothing, of course, is the merchandise line most vital to the retail department store business. Clothing buyers have become probably the most important employees in the retail business. With increased competition from smaller boutiques, larger stores need merchandise that will keep customers coming back. It's up to buyers to get that merchandise into the stores.

GEOGRAPHIC JOB INDEX

The location of retail jobs parallels the distribution of the general population; stores operate where customers live. As an up-and-coming executive in a retail chain, expect to work in a city or suburban area. Most new store construction in the coming years is expected to take place in revitalizing city cores. Department stores are found across the country, with the highest concentration of jobs in the Northeast, Midwest, and West Coast.

If your interest is buying, your geographic options are more limited. For many department store chains, most or all buying takes place in a few key markets, notably New York, NY.

WHO THE EMPLOYERS ARE

A retailer is, in its simplest definition, a third party who sells a producer's goods to a consumer for a profit. The retailing industry as a whole comprises a wide variety of stores of different sizes with different personnel needs. Management personnel are sought by all major retail firms, including grocery, drug, specialty, and variety store chains, but because the most varied opportunities are found in department stores, this chapter focuses on this sector of retailing.

MAJOR EMPLOYERS

Federated Department Stores and Allied Stores Corporation, Cincinnati, OH

Abraham & Straus
Bloomingdales
Bon Marche
Lazarus
Stern's
Rich's

Carter Hawley Hale Stores, Los Angeles, CA
The Broadway
Emporium Capwell
Weinstock's

Dayton Hudson Corporation, Minneapolis, MN
Dayton's
Hudson Stores
Leachmere
Mirvin's
Target Stores

R.H. Macy & Company, New York, NY

Marshall Fields, Chicago, IL

Montgomery Ward & Company, Chicago, IL

J.C. Penney Company, New York, NY

Sears, Roebuck & Company, Chicago, IL

HOW TO BREAK INTO THE FIELD

Your best bet is on-campus interviews. Major retailers actively recruit on college campuses. This is the most accessible way to most potential employers. Don't hesitate, however, to contact employers directly, especially if you want to work for a smaller operation. Read the business section of your newspaper regularly to find out about store expansions, the addition of new stores, or locations and other developments in retailing that can provide important clues to new job openings. Keep in mind that retail or selling experience of any kind will increase your chances of getting hired.

INTERNATIONAL JOB OPPORTUNITIES

Extremely limited. Opportunities to live abroad exist at the corporate level of a few international chains.

ENTREPRENEURIAL DEPARTMENT STORE RETAILING

Chocolate chip cookies next to the fine china? Candy across from the cable-knit sweaters?

Department stores are always looking for products and attractions that entice customers inside their doors. To get those attractions while keeping costs at a minimum, some chains have entered into arrangements with small, independent retailers that specialize in particular products. Essentially, these small retailers lease space inside department stores to sell their wares.

One such entrepreneurial success story is David's Cookies. David's got its start in the 1970's in New York City. Originally a one-storefront operation, David's quickly became a ubiquitous part of the Manhattan street scene, as cookie-hungry patrons discovered the wonders of macadamia-nut chocolate chips, white chocolate chips, and other such tempting morsels.

As David's Cookies grew, its appeal to upscale shoppers wasn't lost on department store moguls. The fit was ideal. Department stores needed high-quality, high-profile offerings to increase patronage, and David's needed an outlet for expansion. So it was that David's entered into a working agreement with the R.H. Macy department store chain, and with its blue-and-white logo set up shop right inside Macy's stores.

STORE MANAGEMENT

If you're a "people person," consider the store management side of merchandising. You'll be responsible for handling the needs of staff and customers.

The job of store management personnel, even at entry level, entails making decisions on your own. But since decisions often have to be made on the spot and involve balancing the interests of both customers and the store, your mistakes are likely to be highly visible. Whether you manage the smallest department or a very large store, you must always keep the bottom line—making a profit—in mind when making decisions.

During training, you will work with experienced managers and will be moved throughout the store to observe all aspects of merchandising. If you're quick to learn and demonstrate management potential, you'll soon be made manager of a small department or assistant manager of a large one. You will have a fair amount of autonomy, but you must stick to store standards and implement policies determined by higher level management.

QUALIFICATIONS

PERSONAL: Ability to learn quickly. Enormous enthusiasm. The flexibility to handle a constantly changing schedule. Willingness to work weekends, holidays, and nights.

PROFESSIONAL: Demonstrated leadership ability. Ability to work with figures, finances, inventories, and quotas. A sense of diplomacy.

CAREER PATHS

LEVEL	JOB TITLE	EXPERIENCE NEEDED
Entry	Department manager trainee	College degree
2	Group department manager	2–3 years
3	Assistant store manager	5–10 years
4	Store manager	8–12 years

JOB RESPONSIBILITIES ♦ ENTRY LEVEL

THE BASICS: Handling staff scheduling. Dealing with customer complaints. Doing plenty of paperwork.

MORE CHALLENGING DUTIES: Monitoring and motivating your sales staff. Assisting in the selection of merchandise for your department. Making decisions and solving problems.

MOVING UP

Advancement in store management depends on how well you shoulder responsibility and take advantage of opportunities to learn. Effectively leading your staff, moving merchandise, and, above all, turning a profit, will secure your promotion into higher levels.

Your first management position will be overseeing a small department, handling greater volumes of money and merchandise. The group department manager directs several department managers, coordinating store operations on a larger scale. From here you might progess to assistant store manager and store manager. This last position is, in may respects similar to running a private business. The best may then go on to the corporate level.

PROMOTIONS

Relocation is often necessary in order to win promotions. Switching store locations every three years or so is not uncommon. However, depending on the chain, a change of workplace need not require a change of address; often stores are within easy driving distance of each other. But the larger the chain, the greater the possibility that you'll have to move to a different city to further your career.

BUYING

Do you fantasize about a shopping spree in the world's fashion capitals? A few lucky buyers, after years of work and experience, are paid to do just that when they're sent to Hong Kong, Paris, or Milan to select new lines of merchandise. Most do not make it to such heights, but on a smaller scale, this is the business of buying.

A buyer decides which goods will be available in a store. Buyers authorize merchandise purchases from wholesalers and set the retail prices. A sensitivity to changing trends, tastes, and styles and an ability to understand and forecast the preference of your own store's customers is crucial. Buyers must also maintain standards of quality while keeping within certain ranges of affordability.

The buyer who works for a discount department store faces a particularly tough job. Obtaining lower-than-average prices for quality merchandise is a real challenge and requires an unerring eye and an ability to negotiate with sellers.

Astute buying translates into profits for the store and advancement for your career. Learning how to spend large sums of money wisely takes practice. Fortunately, as a new buyer you can afford to make a few mistakes, even an occasional expensive one, without jeopardizing your career. A good buyer takes calculated risks, and as you gain experience more of your choices will succeed.

During training, you'll work immediately as an assistant to an experienced buyer. The trainee progresses by observing, asking questions, and offering to take on appropriate responsibilities.

QUALIFICATIONS

PERSONAL: An interest in changing trends and fashions. An ability to work with a wide variety of personalities. A willingness to channel creativity into a commercial enterprise.

PROFESSIONAL: Financial and negotiating know-how. Organizational skills. Good judgment in spotting trends and evaluating products.

CAREER PATHS

LEVEL	JOB TITLE	EXPERIENCE NEEDED
Entry	Assistant or junior buyer	College degree and store training
2	Buyer (small lines)	2–5 years
3	Buyer (large lines)	4–10 years
4	Corporate merchandise manager	15+ years

JOB RESPONSIBILITIES ◆ ENTRY LEVEL

THE BASICS: Assisting your supervising buyer. Placing orders and speaking with manufacturers by phone. Supervising the inspection and unpacking of new merchandise and overseeing its distribution.

MORE CHALLENGING DUTIES: Becoming acquainted with various manufacturers' lines. Considering products for purchase. Evaluating your store's needs. Keeping an eye on the competition.

MOVING UP

Advancement depends on proof of your ability to judge customer needs and to choose saleable goods. The only purchases closely scrutinized by higher authorities are those inconsistent with past practices and standards.

After completing your training, you will first buy for a small department, then, as you become seasoned, for larger departments. High-placed buyers make decisions in buying for a key department common to several stores, for an entire state, or possibly for many stores. Your buying plans must always be well-coordinated with the needs of store management.

FASHION COORDINATION

The job of fashion coordinator exists only in some large department stores. The coordinator takes over part of the role held by buyers in most stores by offering advice to the buying staff on changing tastes, trends, and styles. Where fashion coordinators are employed, they work with the buying staff to ensure that the store's merchandise is completely up-to-date. Although fashion coordination staffs tend to be small, this specialized area allows art majors to exercise their visual talents in an exciting way.

In most cases, fashion coordination is not a career path job in the traditional sense. Although recent graduates may find entry-level jobs as assistants, more often retail personnel move into fashion coordination from merchandising or other areas. To vie for this exciting position you must be able to demonstrate your talents through an exceptional portfolio, which should include examples of fashion design. However, fashion coordinators are not the "artsy" people of the retail industry. Their decisions must be grounded in a solid business sense and an understanding of customer needs.

As in buying, travel can be an important part of the job, especially in a department that sells imported goods. Domestic manufacturers will usually send their own representatives to introduce product lines, but overseas producers expect American retailers to come to them. In some cases, this can mean up to five months a year spent in Asia or Europe. You will probably work harder on your travels than when you are in the store, but you will be treated royally by producers anxious to make a sale.

Because this is such a small area, personal contacts with decision makers in the industry and a proven reputation in the retail business are essential to landing such a position.

DISPLAY

Like fashion coordinating, display is a specialized area employing talented people with art backgrounds. Each season brings the need for new merchandise presentations that must grab the eye of the shopper or passerby. Display people design and implement the window decorations and interior displays that are so important in promoting sales.

Smaller stores will often handle their display needs through outside agencies or freelancers, but career opportunities exist with many large retailers. Display is a small field with low turnover, so openings are quite limited.

As in all retail positions, the recent graduate begins as an apprentice or assistant, and professional skills are learned entirely on the job. Display efforts are coordinated with store management. The department managers are ultimately responsible for the appearance of their sales floors and know the merchandise well, so their input is crucial.

Good display requires more than creativity and originality. Its greatest challenge is working within limitations of time, space, and money. Although more removed from business concerns than other areas of retailing, display personnel must have an appreciation of changing styles—both in the look of merchandise and in the way it is presented to the public.

ADDITIONAL INFORMATION

SALARIES

Entry-level salaries range from $16,000 to $25,000 a year, depending on the employer and the geographic location of the store. Junior buyers tend to be among the best paid entry-level employees.

The following salary ranges show typical annual salaries for experienced retail personnel. In merchandising and fashion coordination, salaries vary with the size and importance of your department.

2–4 years:	$20,000–30,000
5–10 years:	$30,000–45,000
12 years or more:	$40,000 and up

WORKING CONDITIONS

HOURS: Most retail personnel work a five-day, 40-hour week, but schedules vary with different positions. In store management, daily shifts are rarely nine to five, because stores are open as many as 12 hours a day, seven days a week. Night, weekend, and holiday duty are unavoidable, especially for newcomers. Operations personnel work similar hours. Buyers, fashion coordinators, and display people have more regular schedules and are rarely asked to work evening and weekend hours.

ENVIRONMENT: In merchandising, your time is divided between the office and the sales floor, more often the latter. Office space at the entry level may or may not be private, depending on the store. Whether you share space or not, expect to be close to the sales floor. Merchandising is no place for those who need absolute privacy and quiet in order to be productive.

Expect to find yourself in similar surroundings in fashion coordination and display.

WORKSTYLE: In store management, office time is 100 percent work. Every valuable moment must be used effectively to keep on top of the paperwork. On the floor you will be busy overseeing the arrangement of merchandise, meeting with your sales staff, and listening to customer complaints. Long hours on your feet will test your patience and endurance, but you can never let the weariness show. In buying and fashion coordination, office time is spent with paperwork and calls to manufacturers. You might also review catalog copy and illustrations. On the sales floor, you'll meet with store personnel to see how merchandise is displayed and, most important, to see how the customers are responding. Manufacturers' representatives will visit to show their products, and you might spend some days at manufacturer and wholesaler showrooms. Because these jobs bring you into the public eye, you must be well dressed and meticulously groomed. The generous discounts that employees receive as a fringe benefit help defray the cost of maintaining a wardrobe.

Display personnel spend time meeting with management personnel to formulate display plans. You will set up in-store displays during times of light business, so you won't interfere with shoppers.

TRAVEL: In most job areas, your responsibility lies with your own department and your own store; travel opportunities are virtually nonexistent, except for some top-level personnel. Buyers and fashion coordinators are exceptions. Here you may make annual trips to New York, NY, and other key cities. You might also travel to trade shows in which your type of merchandise is displayed.

EXTRACURRICULAR ACTIVITIES/WORK EXPERIENCE

Leadership in campus organizations
Treasurer or financial officer of an organization
Sales position on the yearbook or campus newspaper
Summer or part-time work in any aspect of retailing

INTERNSHIPS

Arrange internships with individual stores or chains; many are eager to hire interns, preferring students who are in the fall semester of their senior year. Check with your school's placement or internship office or with the store itself in the spring for a fall internship. Summer internships are also available with some stores. Contact the placement office or the personnel departments of individual stores for details.

RECOMMENDED READING

BOOKS

Opportunities in Retailing Careers by Roslyn Dolber, NTC Publishing Group: 1989

Contemporary Retailing, *Third Edition* by William H. Bolen, Prentice-Hall: 1988

Directory of Department Stores and Mail Order Firms by the editors of Chain Store Guide, Lebhar Friedman Inc.: revised periodically

Macy's for Sale by Isadore Barmash, Weidenfeld & Nicolson: 1989

Retail Management: A Strategic Approach, Fourth Edition, by Barry Berman and Joel R. Evans, McGraw-Hill: 1989

PERIODICALS
Advertising Age (weekly), Crain Communications, 740 North Rush Street, Chicago, IL 60611

Journal of Retailing (quarterly), New York University, Stern School of Business, 40 West 4th., rm. 202, New York, NY 10003

Stores (monthly), National Retail Merchants Association, 100 West 31st Street, New York, NY 10001

Women's Wear Daily (daily), Fairchild Publications, Inc., 7 East 12th Street, New York, NY 10003

PROFESSIONAL ASSOCIATIONS

American Retail Federation
1616 H Street, N.W.
Washington, DC 20006

National Retail Merchants Association
100 West 31st Street
New York, NY 10001

INTERVIEWS

**FASHION COORDINATOR
MAJOR DEPARTMENT STORE
NEW YORK, NY**

My first job was far removed from retailing—I taught high school math for a year. The school environment really didn't excite me and I felt I could get more from a job. I saw an ad for the position of fashion coordinator at a branch of Gimbels' department store. I wasn't planning a career in retailing, but because I kept up with fashion and felt I had a flair for it, I applied. I got the job and enjoyed the work, but that particular branch was not a high-caliber store, and after two years I was ready to move on.

I took a part-time job as an assistant manager at an Ann Taylor store, one of a chain selling women's clothing. At that time I was also going to school to finish an art degree. My job included store management and some limited buying. I wound up managing my own store, but because Ann Taylor has a small management staff, I felt there wasn't enough growth potential. I came to know the man who was doing store design for the chain. He was expanding his operations and needed help, so I went to work with him. I designed store interiors and fixtures, which gave me a whole new perspective on the industry. I have been lucky to see so many sides of retailing, but these job changes also required me to relocate.

When I moved into fashion coordination with my present employer about seven years ago, I finally found what I had been looking for—a high-powered, high-pressured environment. When I walk into the store each morning I feel that things are moving, happening. That's the fun of retailing.

My responsibility is to work with the buyers, helping them choose the right styles. After you've been in retailing a number of years, you know where fashion has been and you can see where it's going. You decide, really by making educated guesses, what the public will want a year from today. My job includes a lot of travel—

usually eight or nine weeks a year. Where there are products abroad, we explore them. That's the only way to keep up with the competition.

In buying we speak of hundreds of dozens, so you must be volume-oriented. You ask, "What does our regular customer want to see?" Then you make a decision that has to be more right than wrong. I work with children's wear, a department that rarely sees radical changes in style. But there are always new trends in color and design, and new products.

One of the toughest parts of my job is training new buyers and helping with their first big buys. They are understandably nervous about spending several hundred thousand dollars. The fashion co-ordinator is one with buying experience. You offer better advice if you understand the pressure and monetary responsibility of the buyer's job.

Even though I'm in a creative area, business and financial concerns are of the highest importance. You must have a head for business in every retailing job. You want to find beautiful quality products, but if they don't sell, you've failed.

The one drawback to my job is advancement. My talents and experience are best used right where I am now. Unlike the buyers, I really have no place higher to go. But I enjoy my work. I suppose it's like being an artist, and how many artists are really appreciated?

SUSAN HARRINGTON
BLOOMINGDALE'S DEPARTMENT STORE
NEWTON, MA

I was a flight attendant my first two years out of college. The company went bankrupt. I had an opportunity to go to a larger airline carrier, but I decided I didn't want to be a flight attendant for the rest of my life. It's easier to make a career change in your early twenties than 10 or 15 years later. I took a job selling cosmetics over the counter at a department store. They told me that even though I had a four year degree, everyone starts on the counter. After about eight months I felt discouraged. I had been the top salesperson consistently, but there was no promotion on the horizon. Looking back at it now, with a little more professional maturity, I can see that, although every company likes to promote on the basis of merit, if there is no opening or a job they can't always create one for you. I think retail is like advertising and a lot of other occupations that sound glamourous. The pyramid narrows dramatically once you get beyond the entry level. There's a lot of people who want top positions who are qualified for them.

I worked in a retail position in a department store that also had a lot of vendor support with the idea that I could either grow with the store or with the vendor. This didn't happen so I worked at MCI in telemarketing sales and strangely enough, the woman who had been my counter manager for the cosmetics vendor was recruited by another cosmetics company. She hired me to work on her special sales team for a year and a half. I then went to being a personnel consultant for a personnel agency for a year and a half. I wasn't interested in this as a career, but I needed it on my résumé. And from there I got this job because of my retail experience.

Unless you are one of the few who get a position in a management trainee program out of college—and these positions are very limited because we only recruit from a certain list of schools—you take a sales position. My employer offers a lucrative opportunity because our people work on straight commission. While you are waiting to get your foot in the door at least you can make some money. Your initiative and your productivity determines your salary. We feel that these jobs are appropriate for people with a four year degree. Unfortunately most people with a four year degree are not realistic about their position and salary potential. The track here is to go from being a salesperson to being a DMT (Department Manager in Training) to being a Department Manager to being a Divisional, who oversees Department Managers, and from there being a Store Manager. This is your local option. All the buying opportunities are out of New York.

People move up this career path based on their merits. We look for people who are realistic, dedicated, and pay attention to detail. We are interested in people who are providing exceptional customer service. We want people to treat this job like a professional sales opportunity. People who treat their customers like special clients, call them on the phone, write them notes, let them know about special events, and invite them in to shop by appointment. If you are interested in department store retailing there is a lot of opportunity, and something like the commission system at our store can increase your earning potential tremendously.

TOM WENSINGER
COORDINATOR OF EXECUTIVE RECRUITMENT
NEIMAN-MARCUS
DALLAS, TX

I was recruited from campus. I graduated from Texas A & M about four years ago and I went right into the executive development program here at Neiman-Marcus. Recently I took this job where I do the recruitment for that program. Before, I was an assistant buyer in the Men's Division and an assistant buyer in the Ladies Shoe Division.

Our merchandise divisions are centralized, so we do all of our purchasing out of Dallas for stores across the country. Now that doesn't mean that we buy all of our merchandise here in Dallas, but the offices are here and all these activities are coordinated from here. A lot of the assistant buyer's job is communication with department managers across the country, relaying strategies about merchandise flow. All of the day-to-day activities that require input from the buying office more often than not go through the assistant buyer. Also, the assistant buyer's job is very much apprentice oriented in that by the time you accomplish your role as assistant buyer you should be a buyer. That is the goal of being an assistant buyer.

As a coordinator of executive recruitment I am responsible for the hiring and placement of all people within the executive development program. Upon completion of this program I place them in their first job as an assistant buyer. Just like buying goes beyond buying, recruiting goes beyond recruiting. More often than not you do a lot of support work in department store retailing. For instance, you have to have a marketing orientation as an assistant buyer. You are a product manager. For all this merchandise that your buyer is buying, you have to do a lot of analysis to see what is selling, what needs to be moved, what is not selling, what are the costs, what's the most effective way to distribute the merchandise.

Performance is the best way to move up in department store retailing. Advancement is dependent upon the company you work with and how they are willing to promote you. You have to get with a company that's willing to take a risk on you, and along with that risk they've got to give you an opportunity. Making people assistant buyers is risky, but the job has a lot of opportunity because the assistant buyer can exercise a lot of authority—more authority than you would get in a lot of jobs. Your authority develops individually. Somebody who comes right out of the training program won't have a lot of authority. They develop that after a couple of years on the job. Your authority grows as you develop to make buys. Your buyer works with you and lets you select the merchandise. You have the authority to transfer merchandise and make cost related decisions between stores. You negotiate with vendors. There's also a lot of clerical and office work.

I'd want a job applicant to be bright. I'd want them to demonstrate a history of success in whatever they had done. I don't think they would have to necessarily have worked in a retail store to be interesting to us. I would just want them to have done well in whatever they did, be it academics, extracurricular activities, leadership, athletics, or work experience. I want them to have valuable work experience. That doesn't mean that busing tables is less valuable than working in a store or doing an internship. A lot of times you learn a lot more busing tables.

For college graduates, I would encourage them to find a training program within the company as opposed to working on the sales floor and working themselves up. The best way to do this is make an appointment with a campus recruiter. If your college doesn't have any recruitment, then you'll have to send out résumés and try to get to see a recruiter. You would be most successful in gaining an interview in the area of the company's headquarters.

Now, don't get me wrong about the value of being on the floor. After you are an assistant buyer at Neiman-Marcus you are promoted to department manager. I think that being out there on the floor as a department manager for two years is completely necessary. But for someone who wants to be a retail executive, a corporate training program will provide the floor experience without building in that extra rung of sales. If you do start in sales, you would work through their individual store management. You get a department manager's position and then you get nominated for the training program. And then we bring them to Dallas and we put them on the buying career path.

My general advice is that this is a fast paced environment, but if you don't love it don't do it. I find that if you don't love retailing, you'll hate it.

HOTEL
MANAGEMENT

Behind the scenes of bustling hotel lobbies, elegant resorts, and well-appointed conference centers are large staffs with a wide and varied range of skills. Salespeople, managers, dietitians, tour packagers, housekeepers—there is a place for these and numerous others in this colorful and challenging industry.

The hotel industry is growing and changing. Cities and regions are promoting tourism as a source of revenue. More foreigners are traveling in the United States. Hotel chains have expanded in the past ten years, both in the United States and abroad. These developments have increased the competition for travelers' dollars and have created countless new jobs. New challenges have been added to many career positions. Hotels can no longer depend on their size and location for custom; they must actively promote and sell their services. Thus, sales, marketing, advertising, and public relations have become as vital as traditional hotel services.

If you're a take-charge person who enjoys planning and supervising, and can juggle the potentially conflicting demands of gracious service and efficient operations, the industry will welcome you. The chance to live and work in different locales appeals to many candidates. Liberal arts and business graduates will find that they can apply their education and personal qualities in:

- ◆ **FRONT DESK OPERATIONS**

- ◆ **FOOD AND BEVERAGE SERVICES**

- ◆ **MARKETING/SALES**

Few people have trouble finding entry-level jobs, and most of these positions lead quickly to better ones if you show initiative and take extra training. Newcomers, however, must be prepared to put in long hours and learn many facets of the trade. On the plus side, there's plenty of opportunity to take on added responsibility and move up the ladder in a variety of ways. Many hotel chains, independent hotels, and resort facilities offer on-the-job training programs that provide the opportunity for liberal arts and business majors to advance and compete with graduates with degrees in hotel and restaurant management.

Like most service-oriented industries, hotels and resorts are dynamic businesses. New technology has already meant that room reservations and financial operations are computerized. Teleconferencing is changing the nature of the convention and conferences areas of the industry, although its impact is not yet clear. This new means of communications is expected to be a strong factor in attracting business clients. Hotels that specialize in conventions may lose room sales because of teleconferencing; on the other hand, both large and small hotels and host teleconferences may well develop additional business.

JOB OUTLOOK

JOB OPENINGS WILL GROW: Faster than average

COMPETITION FOR JOBS: Minimal

NEW JOB OPPORTUNITIES: The concierge, a standby of European service, is beginning to appear in America's better urban hotels.

There are few positions now, but the opportunities are expected to grow. The concierge knows a city inside out, has contacts everywhere, and provides special assistance to guests. A concierge might obtain tickets to a sold-out show, recommend a nearby optician, or locate a boutique with bilingual personnel. This job requires ingenuity and confidence. No training is available, but if the idea appeals to you, you might be able to create such a position for yourself, once you have worked at the front desk and become familiar with the problems and requests that arise. You'd do well to consult a concierge at a major hotel, who may be able to offer some tips on persuading management to let you try your hand.

GEOGRAPHIC JOB INDEX

Hotels of course, are found everywhere. The largest, and some of the most prestigious, are located in and around major convention and tourist centers, such as San Francisco, CA; Miami, FL; Atlanta, GA; Chicago, IL; New York, NY; and Washington, DC. Other important hotels are in resort areas. If you are interested in moving regularly, big domestic and international chains offer the best opportunities for relocation.

WHO THE EMPLOYERS ARE

HOTEL CHAINS are national and international corporations that operate a number of establishments. They offer many customer services and have a multi-tiered management structure. Chains provide good opportunities for advancement, transfer, and travel. Because employees are transferred frequently, you have a better chance of being promoted quickly than you would in an independent hotel. Corporate headquarters jobs, in, for example, marketing, usually go to employees with experience or advanced degrees or both.

MOTELS are smaller establishments than hotels. They normally provide fewer services, and as a result do not offer as many job opportunities. However, motels located within major cities often do provide services approaching those of hotels, and large motel chains employ marketing and sales personnel at their corporate headquarters.

MAJOR EMPLOYERS

HOTEL CHAINS

Americana Hotels & Realty Corporation, Boston, MA
Fairmount Hotel Company, San Francisco, CA
Four Seasons Hotels, Inc., Toronto, ON
Helmsley Hotels, New York, NY
Hilton Hotels Corporation, Beverly Hills, CA
Hyatt Corporation, Chicago, IL
Intercontinental Hotels Corporation, Montvale, NJ
Marriott Corporation, Bethesda, MD
Meridien Hotels, New York, NY
The Sheraton Corporation, Boston, MA
Westin Hotels Company, Seattle, WA

MOTEL CHAINS

Best Western International, Phoenix, AZ
Econo Lodges of America, Inc., Charlotte, NC
Quality Inns, Inc., Silver Spring, MD
Ramada Inc., Phoenix, AZ

HOW TO BREAK INTO THE FIELD

Finding an entry-level job is not too difficult, especially in the service-oriented departments (food service and house management). A résumé and cover letter to the manager of the department that interests you, the same information to the personnel department, and a follow-up call is the way to start. You will be competing with graduates of hotel/restaurant management training programs. The more challenging entry-level positions often go to people with this targeted education. You must demonstrate your willingness to learn the hotel business from the bottom up.

To become familiar with hotel work and to make contacts, find out from the local convention bureau when large conventions are coming to town and where they will be headquartered. Then contact the hotel and offer to work part-time on the front desk during the convention. You might also make advance contact with convening associations and offer to help in the hospitality booth or in the press room. In addition, a hotel may also need extra help during peak seasons.

INTERNATIONAL JOB OPPORTUNITIES

Possibilities for overseas work exist in the international hotel chains, but you need to prove your competence in the United States first. If you are fluent in a foreign language and have several years of front desk experience, you have a good chance of being transferred abroad.

ENTREPRENEURIAL

A growing number of hotel management professionals are striking out on their own, albeit on a smaller scale. They're putting their experience to work in their own bed and breakfast inns.

B&Bs offer budding entrepreneurs a way to enter the hotel business with a relatively low investment. They are family-run businesses, either private residences where the owners let spare bedrooms for overnight guests, or small inns. Breakfasts, ranging from continental to full eggs-and-bacon repasts, are provided. Some places offer other meals. The attractions for the traveler are apparent: generally lower cost and a "home away from home" atmosphere. For the entrepreneur, the benefits are a more easily manageable, smaller scale operation and an opportunity to deal personally with guests.

The key to a successful B&B is, of course, location. Most bed and breakfasts are found in traditional resort and tourist spots—the Sonoma and Napa valleys of northern California; the Williamsburg area of Virginia; Cape Cod, Martha's Vineyard, and Nantucket in

Massachusetts. Local historic and cultural attractions, beautiful countryside, and seasonal sports activities are all features you'll need to consider when scouting locale.

There are a number of bed and breakfast associations in the U.S., including the Tourist House Association of America (R.D. 2, Box 355A, Greentown, PA 18426). Contact them for further information on opening your own B&B.

FRONT DESK OPERATIONS

The hotel personnel with whom guests come into personal contact comprise the so-called front of the house. They include the door attendant, the bellhop, and the front desk clerk, as well as the individuals who supervise their activities. They play a key role in the hotel's image, and because repeat business is vital to the industry, they must provide consistently excellent service.

Often called the nerve center, the front desk handles the needs of the guests from arrival to check-out. This experience gives the desk clerk a good understanding of the hotel's customers and what they expect in the way of service. Also, the desk clerk learns to cooperate with other employees in the common purpose of efficiently and readily meeting the guests' needs.

Traditionally, the front house has been the starting place for employees whose sights are set on becoming general manager—the executive responsible for all the activities of the hotel. With desk experience behind you, you are able to direct a variety of large staffs and set policies concerning the inner workings of the hotel.

The general manager was once concerned primarily with the needs of the average guest. This concern is still important, but the general manager's responsibilities have now become so broad that supervisors from the sales or the beverage and food divisions can move into this top position. The ideal general manager is one who has had supervisory experience in all areas of the hotel business. The front desk is still the best place to start if you plan to move into top management, but you must be prepared to seize every opportunity to expand the depth and breadth of your experience within the entire industry.

There is no set career path from the entry-level position to the top because each hotel or chain has its own departmental divisions and personnel structures. Before moving into a mid-management position, almost any candidate would go through a six-month to one-year training program. After that, hotel employees might spend up to six years in various supervisory assistantships before earning a more elevated title. The length of time in each position varies according to the size and structure of the hotel or chain, and your willingness and ability to move into new areas.

QUALIFICATIONS

PERSONAL: Energetic. A friendly disposition. A sense of diplomacy. Self-assurance. Common sense. The ability to make quick decisions and to work independently.

PROFESSIONAL: Clerical skills. Bookkeeping may be helpful.

CAREER PATHS

LEVEL	JOB TITLE	EXPERIENCE NEEDED
Entry	Front desk clerk or room clerk	College degree
2	Assistant manager, front office	2–4 years
3	Senior manager, front office	4–6 years
4	Rooms division supervisor	7–10 years
5	Assistant hotel manager	15 + years
6	General manager	20 + years

JOB RESPONSIBILITIES ♦ ENTRY LEVEL

THE BASICS: Take reservations. Assign rooms. Register guests. Handle room keys. Answer questions. Relay messages.

MORE CHALLENGING DUTIES: Supervising clerks, cashiers, and night auditors. Training personnel.

MOVING UP

After you have proven your commitment, learned basic hotel operations, and gained an understanding of the guests' needs, you will be an ideal candidate for assistant manager in the front office. Your promotion will come more quickly if you have from time to time taken the initiative to gain extra responsibility and experience. The assistant acts as a liaision between the desk clerks and the front office manager. As front officer manager, you spend most of your time directing your personnel, but handling major complaints from customers remains an inescapable part of the job. Depending on the size and structure of the hotel, you might move into other supervisory positions, such as rooms division supervisor, in charge of reservations and housekeeping. As you become qualified for higher level management jobs, you may well find that your chances of reaching that level are improved if you change employers.

FOOD AND BEVERAGE SERVICES

Conventions, banquets, conferences, and other group affairs are important sources of a hotel's income. This department arranges everything from wedding receptions and high school proms to major business, political, or social gatherings involving hundreds or even thousands of guests. The responsibilities include scheduling the events, assigning physical facilities, planning and arranging meals and such special services as additional security, extra staff, and press accommodations. The convention and banquet services department stage manages these events, cooperating closely with the customer's representatives—a job that might be purely simple and routine or a herculean task.

The department is also in charge of the hotel's dining rooms, bars, and coffeeshops, which are open to the public and operated as any independent restaurant or cocktail lounge. Managing these facilities requires close and constant supervision of a large and active staff of waiters, chefs, and others.

Duties are extremely varied in this department. Working here gives you an excellent grounding in business management, supervision of extensive staff, and dealing with emergencies smoothly and with dispatch. You must be very well organized, almost unflappable, and able to keep several balls in the air at once.

If you do not have a hotel/restaurant management degree and you aspire to a mid-managerial position in a large hotel, you would have to enter a training program to learn the responsibilities of the kitchen steward, the chef, and the purchasing manager, and their staffs. Career paths vary greatly. They depend on the size and number of the hotel's facilities, and on your own talents and plans.

QUALIFICATIONS

PERSONAL: Outgoing, energetic personality. Creativity. Appreciation of customer's tastes. Organizational ability. Ability to think on your feet.

PROFESSIONAL: Business knowledge. Familiarity with kitchen and dining room procedures. Ability to uphold standards of quality on a daily basis.

CAREER PATHS

LEVEL	JOB TITLE	EXPERIENCE NEEDED
Entry	Trainee	College degree
2	Assistant supervisor of food, beverage, or banquet division	6 months–1 year
3	Supervisor	3–5 years

| 4 | Assistant to food and beverage director | 6–8 years |
| 5 | Food and beverage director | 10–15+ years |

JOB RESPONSIBILITIES ♦ ENTRY LEVEL

THE BASICS: Assigning table-seating arrangements. Learning the menu. Handling last-minute problems.

MORE CHALLENGING DUTIES: Booking groups. Suggesting menus for group functions. Planning logistics. Developing budgets and marketing and advertising strategies.

MOVING UP

After you understand the operations of a particular area (banquet services, for example) you move up to assistant supervisor and begin to train for a management position. Your basic function will be assisting your supervisor, but you will be using salesmanship as well to help promote the restaurant or the banquet and convention facilities with special deals and advertising. An ability to deal effectively and quickly with the needs and grievances of guests and clients is paramount.

After two or three years you would advance to supervisor, managing personnel and coordinating your division. In most major hotels, food services, beverage services, and banquet services are separate, although interrelated functions.

If you have food service experience and have proven your managerial skills, you might choose to work in catering services. The catering manager works closely with groups and associations, serving their special needs. You may provide something as simple as a small wine and cheese reception or as elaborate as a five-course banquet.

With a solid background of experience, you are eligible for advancement to assistant director and director of food and beverage services, supervising this entire division of the hotel. These jobs involve the overseeing of personnel, purchasing and inventory control, monitoring cleanliness and quality, and some advertising and promotion.

Moving up requires a demonstration of initiative—visiting competitors, for example, seeing their methods, and getting ideas to improve your own operations. Because food and beverage services, like front house operations, is a service-oriented function, the customers are everything. Talk with them, discover their needs, listen to their complaints and compliments, and apply what you learn.

MARKETING/SALES

An increased emphasis on this function goes hand-in-hand with the growing competition among hotel chains. The marketing and sales department is responsible for many of the special offers and promotions that attract guests. For example, many hotels have devised schemes to draw business travelers—everything from discounts to free breakfasts and complimentary copies of *The Wall Street Journal.* It is especially important that hotels attract large travel groups and conventions because these are important sources of income. Salespeople are responsible for presenting an appealing package to these potential clients. Often just selling the hotel is not enough, you must also sell its location and special features. Although the hotel may have exceptional facilities, it is competing with many others of comparable quality. Local amenities, atmosphere, and convenience to transportation are discussed along with cost and the client's individual needs. Using these starting points, you must hit on a way to present your hotel and your city persuasively. Creativity, flexibility, and the power to persuade are the keys to success.

Recent graduates enter this department as sales trainees. Once you have an overview of the hotel and convention industries (which might take several months), you become an account executive and start working with clients.

QUALIFICATIONS

PERSONAL: Energetic, sociable personality. Ability to persuade others. Analytic skills. Insight into human nature. Persistence.

PROFESSIONAL: Business sense. Aptitude for numbers. Knowledge of computers and teleconferencing helpful but not essential. Sales or public relations experience often preferred.

CAREER PATHS

LEVEL	JOB TITLE	EXPERIENCE NEEDED
Entry	Sales trainee	College degree
2	Account executive	6 months–1 year
3	Group sales manager	3–7 years
4	Area sales manager	10+ years
5	Marketing and sales manager	15+ years

JOB RESPONSIBILITIES ♦ ENTRY LEVEL

THE BASICS: Calling on associations, large groups, and travel agencies to interest them in the facility you represent. Maintaining accounts. Representing your hotel/resort and city at trade shows. Analyzing your facility and the competition. Giving tours of your hotel.

MORE CHALLENGING DUTIES: Handling group sales. Creating and presenting bids. Overseeing marketing plans and advertising. Writing promotional literature.

MOVING UP

As an account executive, you'll start with local groups and work up to handling national organizations, whose needs are more complex.

The group sales manager supervises the account executives and is in charge of dealing with more prestigious associations and groups.

The area sales manager handles a particular territory, which in sales language is a specific type of organization—sports, youth, trade associations.

The marketing/sales manager is in charge of the entire department and approves the bids created by the account executives. It takes experience and some daring to set a price that is high enough to be profitable yet lower than the competition's. You must be sure, as well, that the hotel can deliver all the promised services. Hotel marketing and sales managers often work with tourist bureaus and local government officials to promote their city or region.

To move up, you must cope with different personalities and deal with office and city politics. You also need confidence, a fresh outlook, and the knowledge of costs and contingencies that equips you to create competitive bids. In this department, the most successful professionals are those with the personality and persistence to sell the hotel, the city, and, above all, themselves.

ADDITIONAL INFORMATION

SALARIES

It is difficult to characterize salaries in the hotel industry because pay is determined by the size, prestige, and location of the hotel. Perks, such as discounts on meals, discounts at chain-affiliated hotels (if you work in the chain), bonuses, and profit-sharing plans, add to your base pay. General managers and, less often, other top managers may receive housing.

Entry-level salaries vary widely—from as low as $17,000 a year. The highest salaries usually go to graduates of hotel/restaurant management programs. Front house personnel also tend to be better paid than those in other departments.

An assistant departmental manager may earn from $25,000 to

$45,000 a year; a departmental manager may earn $70,000 per year or more. The general managers of the most prestigious urban hotels may receive annual compensations close to $100,000.

WORKING CONDITIONS

HOURS: In front house operations and food and beverage services, expect changing shifts that include night hours and weekend work. The hours in these sections of the industry are never routine because the hotel and its banquet facilities are open beyond normal business hours. Management personnel in both areas are used to overtime; they may work a 70-hour week during a major convention. The marketing and sales department tends to keep regular hours, although overtime is common as you adapt your working hours to your clients' needs.

ENVIRONMENT: The desk clerk is in public view most of the time, stationed at the reception desk. Front house managers have offices, but the nature of your work will keep you moving throughout the hotel a great deal of the time. In banquet services, the restaurant becomes a second home. Food services personnel have offices, but these are often small and not far from the noise of the kitchen and the restaurant. In sales and marketing, entry-level personnel often share work space, but since it is removed from the public areas of the hotel the work environment is quieter and less hectic than in front house or food and beverage services.

WORKSTYLE: Your job as a desk clerk means that you are in extensive and continual contact with guests, both over the phone and face-to-face. At peak times, such as morning check-out, the pace can be hectic. Evening hours tend to be calmer. In banquet services, you will be consistently on the move: supervising staff, meeting customers, making arrangements, and showing the hotel's facilities. Sales and marketing are desk jobs. In sales, expect a great deal of phone work and many meetings.

TRAVEL: In national chains, opportunities exist for management personnel in all areas to visit member hotels to exchange ideas and experiences. Sales and marketing personnel could travel nationally (and even internationally) in their quest to attract convention, tour groups, and other new business, but not usually at entry level. Management personnel, particularly in sales, can be temporarily moved to newly opened hotels to help their staffs begin functioning.

Hotel chains often try to foster an international image, so temporary assignments overseas are not uncommon for desk clerks who speak a foreign language. Such experience can speed your progress in hotels with large foreign clienteles.

EXTRACURRICULAR ACTIVITIES/WORK EXPERIENCE

Work at a campus pub, student center or cafeteria
Part-time work in a hotel, restaurant or catering business
Planning social functions for dorms, fraternities, sororities, and clubs
For sales and marketing: Selling ads for school publications
Part-time sales work

INTERNSHIPS

Most formal internship programs offered by hotels are geared primarily toward students majoring in hotel management. Therefore, you must investigate internship possibilities on your own and must convince prospective sponsors that you are sincerely interested in a hotel career and can be useful to their operation. Your chances of being accepted as an intern in front desk operations or banquet facilities are improved if you have hotel or restaurant experience. Even a stint as a part-time waiter is valuable if it gives you a chance to observe the operation of a quality restaurant. If you are interested in an internship in sales and marketing, be sure to play up sales experience you have had in any area.

RECOMMENDED READING

BOOKS

Directory of Hotel and Motel Systems, American Hotel and Motel Association. This annual directory lists hotel and motel chains and their properties.

See also various other books published by the Educational Institute of the American Hotel and Motel Association; for example, *Sanitation Management: Strategies for Success*, 2nd ed., 1990; *Training for the Hospitality Industry*, 2nd ed., 1989.

PERIODICALS

Lodging and Food-Service News (monthly), 131 Clarendon Street, Boston, MA 02116

Lodging Hospitality (monthly), 111 Chester Avenue, Cleveland, OH 44114

PROFESSIONAL ASSOCIATIONS

American Bed and Breakfast Association
16 Village Green
Suite 203
Crofton, MD 21114

American Hotel and Motel Association
888 Seventh Avenue
New York, NY 10019

Council on Hotel, Restaurant, and Institutional Education
311 First Street, N.W.
Suite 700
Washington, DC 20001

Educational Foundation of the National Restaurant Association
20 North Wacker Drive
Suite 2620
Chicago, IL 60606

Hotel Sales and Marketing Association International
1300 L Street, N.W.
Suite 800
Washington, DC 20005

INTERVIEWS

DIRECTOR OF SALES AND MARKETING
MAJOR HOTEL CHAIN

I majored in marketing at the University of New Hampshire because
I wanted to go into sales. After graduation I was hired by the
Dunfey Corporation and went through its year-long training program. I was assigned to sales, the department that interested me,
and began as an entry-level account executive. After I rotated
through various departments to acquire a general knowledge of the
hotel, I began going out on calls with an experienced salesperson.
Once I had the right style and approach, I went out on my own.

My first job was at the Berkshire Place, a Dunfey hotel in New
York City. I advanced to a group sales manager and then became
tour and travel sales manager. I then moved to Boston, and became
a sales manager with my current employer, and have since been
promoted to my present position.

What makes hotel sales different from many other types of sales
is that the product you are selling is intangible—it's your company's
services and its name. Now, as the director of sales and marketing,
I do some market research. I look into who our clientele has been
and what type of customers our competitors are going after. Before
opening a hotel in a new city, we have to find out such things as

what kind of customers we can attract and where the best location is for our hotel. Once we determine that, we try to contact potential clients so that they're aware of our new facility.

To get into the marketing and sales department of a hotel, you must have good organizational skills, an eye for detail, and strong interpersonal skills. That doesn't necessarily mean you have to have a hotel background. The kind of degree you have is less important than the skills you bring to the job.

Despite the image, I wouldn't say that hotel sales is glamorous work, but it is never dull. Everyone in sales has to put in a lot of work. We work weekends and travel often. Sometimes we are dealing with a lot of money, so there's a high excitement level. I especially like the travel that my own work requires and the frequent interaction with people.

On a typical day I devote much of my time to handling our hotel's largest accounts. I keep in touch with them and make phone calls to potential customers. This kind of work demands an aptitude for numbers as well as an understanding of the customer's needs and of how our hotel meets these needs. During the day I do most of my work over the phone and at business luncheons (I often attend as many as four luncheons a week). I usually prepare sales presentations and reports after hours.

As in any profession, you have to deal with a certain amount of politics to get ahead, but in the long run it is your commitment to the job and your selling ability that pays off.

ASSISTANT FRONT OFFICE MANAGER
MAJOR HOTEL CHAIN

When I graduated from the University of New Brunswick with a degree in French literature in 1973, I had no idea of what I wanted to do. When I finally started job hunting, I applied to jobs in radio, film, airlines and hotels. I fell into hotels by accident, because the industry tends to make hiring decisions very quickly. Sometimes you hear on the same day you interview. Nevertheless, a hotel job appealed to me. I wanted a job that was different from the usual nine-to-five routine and one in which I could work with people.

I started at the Queen Elizabeth Hotel in Montreal, which is part of Hilton International, in April 1974. I didn't have a formal training period. I started out by working three days a week as an interviewer in the personnel department and two days as a hostess in the coffeeshop. They were using me to fill holes wherever someone was needed. After a summer in these jobs, I spent a month in catering, a month in public relations, and several months in food and beverage. These were all clerical jobs, but I learned a lot. In April 1975 I became a room clerk, and I stayed at the front desk about a year.

In June 1975 I changed employers. A new Four Seasons hotel was opening in Montreal. A friend who had gone to work there lured me over. Three weeks after that hotel opened, the executive housekeeper left and I was given the job. With no experience in housekeeping, I found myself in charge of keeping the hotel clean, which meant directing the staff, hiring new people, seeing the salespeople who promoted cleaning products, testing these products, and so on.

In August 1977 I went to the Queen Elizabeth Hotel because I missed working for Hilton. I went into the sales department as a meetings coordinator, handling smaller conferences held at the hotel. I then moved up to convention coordinator, handling conventions of 800 rooms with as many as 2000 people.

I was transferred to the Harbour Castle Hilton Hotel in Toronto, staying in convention services at first and then becoming sales manager. I was working with the Canadian market only, which is relatively small. We kept files on all associations in the country, and I solicited their business.

In the summer of 1981 I was transferred to Chicago as sales manager of my current hotel. However, I found the American market to be more competitive, especially at that time, when the recession was hurting the convention business. My personality is such that I wasn't comfortable going to cocktail parties, which is where a lot of sales take place, trying to sell the hotel's services and being aggressive. I fondly remembered my days in the front office: the action, the endless variety, the cohesiveness among the staff. It's the center of things. So I requested a change and became assistant front office manager, a job I still hold.

I think the front desk is really the best place to start in this business. Rooms are what hotels are all about and what makes this business different from any other. Also, rooms are usually the greatest revenue-producing center for a hotel, so it's important to have a good understanding of how the front desk works.

In the past ten years, I've seen a greater emphasis put on hotel degrees, but anyone can enter this business; it may just take longer if you don't have a specialized degree. The people who do best in this business are the ones who like people, are easy-going, and don't get ruffled easily.

MANUFACTURING

The numbers are disheartening, to say the least. In 1970, 90 percent of all the color TVs sold in the United States were made in the United States. By the late 1980's, that figure dipped to 10 percent. In 1970, 40 percent of all audiotape recorders sold in the United States of were American-made. By the late 1980s, no such recorders were being manufactured in this country. United States-based machine tool centers accounted for nearly all such products sold in the United States of in 1970. Less than 20 years later, 65 percent of those sales were lost to overseas manufacturers. The numbers are even worse for telephones—from nearly 100 percent control of the domestic phone market in 1970, American companies' share slipped to 25 percent as the nation emerged from the Reagan years.

When the United States' position as world manufacturing leader first started its decline, few business and economics experts worried. The nation's future was not in jeopardy, they assured. We were just moving from a manufacturing-based economy to a service-based economy. It was a natural economic progression.

A few years and trillions of dollars of trade imbalance later, few such arguments are heard. No less a leading economic light than Lester C. Thurow, dean of the Massachusetts Institute of Technology's Sloan School of Management, has acknowledged that the United States must regain its manufacturing presence.

The attempted rebuilding of the manufacturing sector may well be the toughest and most important task facing the nation as it moves toward the year 2000. Undoubtedly, business planners and analysts will play a major part in the success or failure of that task. Companies are now understandably wary of "bean counters" who are well versed in portfolio theory and quantitative management but who know very little about the specific manufacturing process or market they seek to run. More and more, they will be looking for business experts who have a detailed knowledge of their specific business.

Although the Northeast and Midwest have traditionally been the strongest regions for manufacturing in the United States, the fastest growing areas since the mid-1950's have been the Southwest, the South, and California. The Northeast is known for its concentration of clothing, electronics equipment, food processing, and printing plants; the Midwest for its automotive, heavy industry, iron and steel plants; the Gulf States for petrochemicals; California for high-technology industries, aerospace, and food products; Dallas-Fort Worth, TX, Wichita, KS, and Atlanta, GA, for the aircraft industry.

New developments in technology have had considerable impact on the manufacturing industry. Such advances as automated material handling, robots, and computerized production techniques have made equipment and many long-used manufacturing techniques obsolete. Management and labor have required retraining, and plants have required modernization. Companies that have been unwilling or unable to adapt to the technological changes have found themselves competing unfavorably, both with other American companies and with companies abroad. Rising costs have led a number of companies to relocate their facilities to more rural settings where labor is cheaper and the tax structure more favorable. Furthermore, concern for environmental pollution and energy waste have required management to set up special departments or to hire consultants so that they can make appropriate changes to conform to the law and cut down on energy waste.

◆ MARKETING AND MARKET RESEARCH

◆ FINANCE

Marketing and market research involves maximizing the way in which the company's product is presented in the marketplace; and finance involves managing the company's money and assets for profit and growth. These job functions are discussed in detail later in the chapter. However, two additional functions are noteworthy; industrial relations/human resources management, and procurement and supply. These jobs are in much shorter supply than marketing and finance positions. For jobs in procurement and supply, a technical background can be an advantage.

Because the manufacturing industry is so broad, the discussion in this chapter is limited to five key areas: automobiles, chemicals, food processing, pharmaceuticals, and household products.

JOB OUTLOOK

JOB OPENINGS WILL GROW: As fast as average

COMPETITION FOR JOBS: Keen.

Traditionally, the top manufacturing companies have been extremely selective in choosing new employees. Their criteria are likely to get even tougher as they look for talent to help in their recovery. Some companies concentrate their recruiting efforts exclusively at top-tier business schools. Unsolicited résumés usually stand little change of being noticed. Other companies are less impressed by big-school credentials; they send interviewers and recruiters to more schools across the country. Of course, well-qualified individuals with a strong academic track record and related industrial experience will be at an advantage in the search for entry-level jobs.

NEW JOB OPPORTUNITIES: As manufacturers make the decision to pursue profits through industrial output rather than manipulating paper, job opportunities will become more available. In the automotive industry, job levels are still moderated by the desire to remain "lean and mean" in staff levels, but car makers realize they have an ongoing need to build solid management. Manufacturing plants are being retooled to reduce production costs, turn out more economical cars, and become more competitive in the marketplace.

The chemical industry is making a comeback after some hard times in the 1980's, but plant and personnel levels are still lower than they had been. The agricultural chemical and fertilizer business is picking up, as is the petrochemical sector. Still, the fortunes of the chemical industry can turn dramatically almost overnight, due to such varying factors as government regulation, agribusiness conditions, and environmental regulations.

The food processing industry, which has been witness to a host of mergers and takeovers in recent years, remains strong, although profitability has declined somewhat in the past few years. It remains to be seen whether the merger mania that gripped the industry will abate. Meanwhile, pressure from government and consumer groups to increase product safety and provide more nutrition information is cutting into profits. Despite this pressure, food processors are among the stingiest companies when it comes to research and development spending. In 1988, food processors on the average spent less than 1 percent of their sales revenues on R&D.

The pharmaceutical industry continues to grow steadily as a result of increasing numbers of older citizens and their expanding health needs, increased government funding for health care and medical research, and the introduction of new drugs and health care items.

Problems facing the industry focus on the area of drug approvals. The Food and Drug Administration is being pressured by drug producers to speed up the drug approval process, while consumer pressure groups are agitating to tighten requirements and procedures in the aftermath of several fatalities involving FDA-approved drugs. The industry's emphasis on research and development has resulted in the successful introduction of a record number of new products into the marketplace. Demand for health care equipment is expected to continue, with a strong market in the area of electromedical equipment.

The anticipated growth areas for the household products industry during the next few years include generic brands, heavy-duty liquid laundry detergents, liquid soap, and specialty soaps. Cosmetics and toiletries, natural cosmetics, men's fragrances, and ethnic cosmetics are expected to be strong markets. This industry is especially responsive to advertising, marketing, new product development, and improvement programs as companies vie for a larger share of the market. Government regulations are having an impact on product acceptance as ingredients in soaps, detergents, and cosmetics are subjected to scrutiny for their environmental and consumer safety.

If the manufacturing area that interests you is not covered in this chapter, you may wish to familiarize yourself with it through a number of books, available in your local or college library, that offer excellent listings of professional associations and trade publications. These include *The Ayer Directory of Publications; Business Publications Rates and Data; Encyclopedia of Associations; Magazine Industry Market Place; National Trade & Professional Associations of the United States; Ulrich's International Periodicals Directory;* and *Where to Find Business Information.* Full details can be found under "Recommended Reading" at the end of this chapter.

GEOGRAPHIC JOB INDEX

The leading manufacturing states according to the U.S. Census Bureau are California, Illinois, Indiana, Michigan, New Jersey, New York, Ohio, Pennsylvania, and Texas.

WHO THE EMPLOYERS ARE

AUTOMOBILES are a major manufactured item. This industry produces motor vehicles (buses, passenger cars, and trucks) and auto parts, both original and replacement.

CHEMICALS produced by companies in this industry are basic chemicals (including chlor-alkalis, industrial gases, inorganic and organic chemicals); synthtic materials (including synthetic fibers, plastics, and synthetic rubber); and specific chemical products (such as cosmetics, detergents, drugs, explosives, fertilizers, paints, pesticides, and soaps).

FOOD PROCESSING represents more than 13 percent of the nation's manufacturing output. This industry includes six basic product areas: alcoholic beverages, bakery products, bottled and canned soft drinks, canned and frozen fruits and vegetables, dairy processing, and meat and meat packaging.

PHARMACEUTICALS has been one of the five most profitable industries in the United States for more than 20 years. It includes companies that specialize in prescription (ethical) drugs, over-the-counter (proprietary) drugs, and health care equipment.

HOUSEHOLD PRODUCTS include a wide range of manufactured products from soaps and detergents (the largest group) to bleaches, cleaning compounds, floor waxes, and toiletries.

MAJOR EMPLOYERS

AUTOMOBILES
Chrysler Corporation, Detroit, MI
Ford Motor Company, Dearborn, MI
General Motors Corporation, Detroit, MI

CHEMICALS
American Cyanamid Company, Wayne, NJ
E.I. DuPont DeNemours & Co., Inc., Wilmington, DE
W.R. Grace & Company, New York, NY

FOOD PROCESSING
General Foods Corporation, White Plains, NY
General Mills, Inc., Minneapolis, MN

The Nestlé Company, Inc., White Plains, NY

PHARMACEUTICALS
Merck & Co. Inc., Rahway, NJ
American Home Products Corp., New York, NY
Pfizer Inc., New York, NY

HOUSEHOLD PRODUCTS
The Clorox Company Inc., Oakland, CA
Johnson & Johnson, New Brunswick, NJ
Schering Plough Corporation, Kenilworth, NJ

For additional information on manufacturing companies, several references are particularly helpful. The *Thomas Register of American Manufacturers* offers an extensive multivolume listing of American manufacturers. *The Career Opportunity Index* organizes companies by location in a series of regional editions. An alphabetical employer index, cross-referenced by primary business function and location, highlights approximately 1500 American companies.

HOW TO BREAK INTO THE FIELD

A substantial number of entry-level candidates get their first job through business school placement office referrals and interviews on campus. Major manufacturing corporations are looking for competent people to be managers. If they are impressed with your capability, they will often create a job for you rather than miss the opportunity to emply you. Candidates with previous work experience in the industry and an understanding of its problems have a definite advantage. If you are a first-year business school student and have a preference for a specific industry, contact the company's director of college recruitment or personnel director to inquire about summer employment. Many manufacturing companies offer summer internships to M.B.A. students. This is an excellent opportunity for you to obtain firsthand experience in the industry, get a good idea of what jobs are available, and make valuable contacts for future full-time employment.

College recruiting personnel offer a few tips on interviewing; have a clear idea of your business goals and be able to explain your reasons for wanting to work for that specific company; and be prepared to discuss the area for which you are best suited. Candidates who are vague about their business objectives and display ignorance about the industry and the company interviewing them produce a negative reaction.

If you have high career goals for yourself, be sure to determine the company's basic management orientation when you are looking for your entry-level job. In some companies, the career path to the top is through marketing; in others, finance is the route to follow. If you have executive management aspirations, you may wish to look for a company that emphasizes your specialty in its management structure.

INTERNATIONAL JOB OPPORTUNITIES

Opportunities for international assignments are rare. If you are interested in working overseas, you should seek employment in a company with international divisions. It usually takes three to five years or more of successful job experience before a corporation considers moving an executive to a foreign division.

MARKETING AND MARKET RESEARCH

Marketing and market research provide a critical link to the sales, production, and finance departments of your company. In large corporations, the two job functions are distinct career areas. Market research provides technical expertise in data collection and analysis and is technical in nature. Marketing makes decisions based on market research data and is managerial in orientation. In smaller companies, the two areas may be combined.

As a marketing staff person you will help evaluate every product or service of your company and provide data and recommendations that will maximize the product's acceptance by the consumer. You will help determine whether a new product should be introduced, who is likely to buy it, and what price should be charged. Marketing departments cope with such problems as what features the product should have and how it should be packaged. You will be heavily involved with advertising and public relations, making decisions on how the product should be introduced, what media should be used, and what image of the company should be portrayed. In the case of existing products, you will examine customer attitudes: whether users like the product's design and performance, whether they are having any problems, and what improvements, if any, are needed. Are there additional applications of the product that could be implemented, or new markets to approach? How does the company's market share compare with that of its competitors?

Advances in technology have brought vast quantities of data within easy reach. Modern communications links have shortened the distance from customers to suppliers. Your use of the computer will make it possible to hypothesize, analyze, and apply the results of market studies of product, audience, and price, and ensure that your company is competitive in the marketplace.

QUALIFICATIONS

PERSONAL: Excellent interpersonal skills. Highly motivated. Broad-based background.

PROFESSIONAL: Excellent organizational skills. Good oral and written communications skills. In-depth understanding of business management. Knowledge of statistics. Consumer empathy.

CAREER PATHS

LEVEL	JOB TITLE	EXPERIENCE NEEDED
Entry	Assistant marketing/ product manager	College degree
2	Associate product manager	1–2 years
3	Product manager	3–4 years
4	Product group manager	6 years
5	Category manager	8 years
6	Marketing manager	10–11 years
7	General manager	13–15 years

JOB RESPONSIBILITIES ♦ ENTRY LEVEL

THE BASICS: Writing memos and reports on product performance, customer reaction, or other variables affecting your product. Meeting with package suppliers and designers. Liaison with public relations or advertising department or agency.

MORE CHALLENGING DUTIES: Working on analyses, budgets, and key strategies. Doing volume planning. Assessing competitive position. Developing promotional materials.

MOVING UP

As an associate product manager, you'll be in charge of media plans and overall strategies in the development of advertising. A small brand name product may also be under your supervision.

The next series of advancements will depend not only on your capability to perform well in your job and your readiness to move on, but on openings as well. In a food packaging company, for example, the product manager slot can be the career path to the top positions in the corporation—chairperson or general management executives. As a product manager, your scope of influence will have expanded to put you in charge of setting overall brand strategies and advertising policies for one product or several related brands. The next step up is product group manager, where you will supervise all the activities of the assistant and associate product managers and be responsible for volume, profit, and financial planning for your brands.

Depending on your company's size, management structure, and industry, your next career move might be category manager, marketing manager, and finally general manager. A fast-track person in a major food packaging corporation can move from entry level to division marketing manager in ten years. If you are very competent and the next career slot in marketing is filled, you may be moved into the corporate area for a staff position in marketing.

In larger corporations, the area of market research offers additional career opportunities. Market research involves analysis of marketing and economic data, and developing and conducting studies regarding purchasing attitudes and the company's advertising image. Entry-level candidates begin as market research analysts, progressing to market research manager, group market research manager, and ultimately director of market research. Analysts supervise clerical and data tabulating functions; collaborate with managers on special assignments; and specify studies and provide data for the product business units.

In pharmaceutical or chemical companies, entry-level marketing candidates can look forward to firsthand experience in field sales for three to six months. In some cases, you may serve as sales rep in a territory and spend your first year selling the company's product before returning to the home office for a position as product manager or in market research. If you have an interest in and an aptitude for sales management, you might progress to field sales manager.

FINANCE

Financial personnel are responsible for the economic health of a corporation. They manage the company's money and its tangible and intangible assets, in the context of the capital market, the corporate tax structure, and prevailing economic conditions.

As an associate financial analyst, your analytical ability will help you identify key business problems, evaluate alternatives, and develop logical conclusions and recommendations. You will be involved with budgets, capital expense proposals, financial statements, operating costs, sales forecasts, and long-range plans.

You will find many challenging opportunities within the financial area of the corporation. Using the latest data acquisition techniques and analysis methods, you will interact with research and management areas and work with marketing personnel. You will be involved in many phases of the company's operations, ranging from corporate departments to operating divisions and manufacturing plants. At some firms the new employee is assigned to an experienced staff member who supervises a planned rotation assignment covering such areas as financial analysis, general and cost accounting, marketing accounting, and analysis and financial planning. At other companies you might be assigned to as single area where you are supervised by an experienced analyst.

QUALIFICATIONS

PERSONAL: Confident. Self-motivated. Flexible. Interacts well with people.

PROFESSIONAL: Well-organized. Excellent decision-making skills. Good oral and written communication. Broad understanding of business management. Accounting and computer skills.

CAREER PATHS

LEVEL	JOB TITLE	EXPERIENCE NEEDED
Entry	Associate financial analyst or finance management trainee	College degree
2	Staff financial analyst	1 year
3	Senior analyst	3–5 years
4	Department head	5–7 years
5	Manager	9–10 years
6	Director	12–15 years

JOB RESPONSIBILITIES ♦ ENTRY LEVEL

THE BASICS: Learning the financial structure of the corporation. Writing reports.

MORE CHALLENGING DUTIES: Conducting field audits. Developing and administering budgets. Working with marketing personnel as part of a project team. Initiating special studies. Using computer simulation and forecasting techniques.

MOVING UP

As you move on to staff financial analyst, you will have additional responsibility in organizing and completing jobs. You will continue to do monthly financial reporting and profit planning, but you may be assigned to a different group. You will also help some of the entry-level analysts, assisting them in accomplishing their tasks, and doing some initial training.

You will gain a firmer command of the company's financial structure and operations as you move on to senior analyst. A number of career paths are available at this point. Advancement can be vertical or horizontal—from one financial area to another, or between corporate and divisional units. Depending on your industry, your job might include developing budgets for a manufacturing facility or analyzing the profit potential of future product lines. You might have responsibility for preparing financial data for reports to stockholders. At the department head or manager level you might have the opportunity to move into a smaller affiliate, or be assigned overseas. With each succeeding move you will have a wider span of responsibilities and more people to supervise. If experience with a specific division would be useful at this point in your career, you might be moved from department head to another area of the company and again have the title of senior analyst.

Challenging opportunities are available in the tax departments, treasurer's department, and controller areas of the corporation. If your company has an international division, you could move into international operations, working with financing arrangements, planning currency fluctuations, and planning intercompany transactions.

Many companies encourage employee advancement through a program of workshops and seminars designed to hone financial and management skills. Tuition reimbursement plans are also common for approved courses of study at schools and colleges.

ADDITIONAL INFORMATION

SALARIES

Entry-level salaries for M.B.A.s vary widely in manufacturing. Although the average starting salary is in the range of $30,000 to $35,000 per year, some are as low as $24,000 and as high as $45,000 annually, depending on the company, the industry, the business school you attend, your previous experience, and location. Salary increases depend on performance. Top-level managers in some industries can earn well into six figures.

WORKING CONDITIONS

HOURS: Manufacturing corporations vary in their working hours for management personnel. Many companies formally start work at 7:30 a.m., especially if manufacturing operations are in progress at the same location. Or they may schedule the work day to begin at 8:30 or 9:30 a.m. In still other businesses, executives may work flex-time hours, setting their own eight-hour work day period, with the approval of their supervisors. It is not uncommon for staff to take work home in the evenings or on the weekends, or to work late during rush periods.

ENVIRONMENT: Depending on the size, location, age, and style of your company, and on whether you are working at corporate headquarters, a field sales office, or in a manufacturing plant, your working facilities and equipment will range from plush to traditional to adequate. You may work in a partitioned area that is part of a large, open work center, or you might have your own office with desk, chair, and door. In a factory, the working arrangements could be as informal as a desk tucked into a quiet corner at the end of a hall.

WORKSTYLE: As an entry-level marketing analyst, you can expect to spend a reasonable amount of time at your desk, evaluating reports, generating memos, and talking on the phone. You will need to attend meetings and follow up on details to get the job done.

As a financial analyst, you will spend a lot of time at your desk. Data acquisition may require meetings, phone calls, or access to the computer terminal.

TRAVEL: Local travel will be part of your marketing job, with occasional visits to the ad agency, the printer, or a new product launching site. During your first financial assignment travel will probably be minimal.

INTERNSHIPS

If you have a special interest, expertise, or experience related to a particular company or field of manufacturing, you may write to the director of personnel or the college recruiting department at the company of your choice. It is a good idea to familiarize yourself with the industry and the company and to include your specific reasons for seeking employment with that company. A successful summer internship provides valuable industrial experience, and will be an asset when you are ready to apply for full-time employment. In addition, your summer job may lead to an employment offer from that company when you graduate.

RECOMMENDED READING

BOOKS
The Ayer Directory of Publications, IMS Press: Revised annually

Business Publications Rates and Data, Standard Rate and Data: Revised annually

The Career Opportunity Index, Career Research Systems: Revised semi-annually

Encyclopedia of Associations, Gale Research Company: Revised annually

Magazine Industry Marketplace, R. R. Bowker: Revised annually

M.B.A. Employment Guide, Association of M.B.A. Executives: 1984

National Trade and Professional Associations of the United States, Columbia Books: Revised annually

Standard and Poor's Register of Corporations, Directors and Executives, Standard and Poor: Revised annually

Thomas Register of American Manufacturers, Thomas Publishing Company: Revised annually

Ulrich's International Periodicals Directory, R. R. Bowker: Revised annually

Where to Find Business Information by David M. Brownstone and Gordon Carruth, John Wiley and Sons: 1982

PERIODICALS
Ideas & Solutions (monthly), Box 600927, North Miami Beach, FL 33160

Journal of Manufacturing and Operations Management (4 times/yr.), 52 Vanderbilt Ave., New York, NY 10017

Journal of Product Innovation Management (4 times/yr.), 52 Vanderbilt Ave., New York, NY 10017

Manufacturing Systems (monthly), 25 West 550 Geneva Rd., Wheaton, IL 60188

Marketing Communications (monthly), 50 West 23rd St., New York, NY 10010

Marketing News (bi-weekly), 250 S. Wacker Dr., Chicago, IL 60606

PROFESSIONAL ASSOCIATIONS

American Finance Assocation
Graduate School of Business Administration
New York University
100 Trinity Place
New York, NY 10006

American Financial Services Association
1101 Fourteenth Street, N.W.
Washington, DC 20005

American Management Association
135 West 50th Street
New York, NY 10020

American Marketing Association
Suite 200, 250 South Wacker Drive
Chicago, IL 60606

American Society for Personnel Administration
30 Park Drive
Berea, OH 44017

Association of M.B.A. Executives, Inc.
305 Madison Avenue
New York, NY 10165

Financial Management Association
University of South Florida
Tampa, FL 33620

Institute of Financial Education
111 East Wacker Drive
Chicago, IL 60601

National Association of Manufacturers
1776 F Street, N.W.
Washington, DC 20006

National Association of Purchasing Management
496 Kinderkamack Road
P.O. Box 418
Oradell, NJ 07649

INTERVIEWS

LISA HEID
MANAGER, BENEFITS ADMINISTRATION
ELI LILLY & CO.
INDIANAPOLIS, IN

I had been teaching for three years when I decided to make a job change. After taking a few courses to see if I'd like business, I enrolled as a finance major in a full-time M.B.A. program at Indiana University.

I have been with Eli Lilly for about seven years, and I have held a number of positions in the company. My first job was as associate financial analyst for the pharmaceuticals division. I was one of two analysts doing forecasting and business planning. The job included reporting actual monthly sales, expenses, and income results to management, as well as forecasting those totals for the rest of the year. It involved working with numbers and being able to analyze and explain issues. Computer skills were essential in managing the amount of data required in this type of management reporting. My other responsibilities included budget analysis for the field and home office departments and solving departmental budget problems as they came up.

After one year, I was promoted to staff financial analyst. I remained in the pharmaceuticals division, assuming additional responsibility for coordinating, organizing, and completing projects. Six months later, I moved to a position in pharmaceuticals credit. In that job, I traveled about 10 percent of the time, making visits to wholesalers, performing financial analyses to determine appropriate credit levels, and writing reports. This job provided me with a totally new focus, working with people outside the company, primarily wholesalers and bankers.

After that, I started working in the corporate financial group as a staff financial analyst. My responsibilities included budget analysis for the industrial relations and corporate affairs groups. We got involved in monthly financial reporting and did business planning. In effect, I functioned as a financial consultant for those two groups.

I then became department head of accounting information and reporting. In that position, I was responsible for doing all financial consolidations for Lilly's U.S. operations. That was also my first managerial role. I supervised a staff of four. From there, I moved to manager of medical services, changing from an area of technical expertise to an administrative position. My staff at that point numbered about 50. We were responsible for generating information on our medical products, as well as international product registration.

Currently, I am manager of benefits administration. I and my staff of about 40 human resources professionals are responsible for administering the company's group health, 401(k), and retirement plans. The position provides a good blend of business and finance issues.

Working at Lilly has been a good experience for me. One of the reasons I left the education field was the lack of flexibility. Here I've been able to make changes and take on new challenges. There are crunch periods a few times each month when we work longer hours, but I can schedule my vacations and have time for my own leisure activities. The job doesn't create any undue stress. The important thing is to anticipate some of the things management is going to want. At times it is hectic, but I try to be fairly even in my workstyle. I know I push myself when there's a deadline. At those times I seem to have a higher energy level.

I think the key to job success is feeling that the company you choose is where you want to be. Having a good match is important. A lot depends on the working climate and the people you're working with. If you feel that you're not making a contribution, it can be frustrating. It's important to view your work as meaningful and to see it being utilized by management in the decision-making process.

ASSISTANT MARKETING MANAGER
FOOD PROCESSING COMPANY

When I graduated with my M.B.A. from Columbia University, I was looking for a job that would offer me room for growth, where I could be part of an organization that has clout and power to change things in the market place and bring benefits to the consumer. I was interviewed by a broad range of companies and picked my current employer because it's a large consumer food company with some of the country's leading brands, and it markets its products around the world.

As an assistant marketing manager, I report to the marketing manager in charge of new product development in the beverage area. My job is to work on new products and help bring them to market. I was put in charge of running two test markets for fruit juice-based beverages. I help decide what we want to test and then oversee the implementation: how much product is needed to conduct the test, shelf placement of product, and consumer promotion events. I also visit the markets. I'm responsible for monitoring 20 supermarkets in two cities. I spend a lot of time handling details for our advertising and promotion campaigns. I review mechanicals at the printer to check that they're right. I work with the ad agency to insure that our products are properly represented in photographs. I may make a content decision at a shoot to make sure that the tone of the commercial reflects the proper image of the company and the brand. Overseeing the budget is also my responsibility. I get a list of our actual expenditures and compare this with our estimates. I project costs for the rest of the year on a month-by-month basis, and if we're going to be over budget, I discuss it with my boss and decide how to get back on budget. I also spend a lot of time setting up research focus groups, writing memos, and coordinating other office activities.

One of the great things about my job is that it's so diverse. There's a new challenge every day. You're always meeting and working with people. My company doesn't have a formal training program. It's more like a "deep water policy"; they throw you in and see if you can swim! Like any good job, it's fairly high-pressured. There are good days and bad days when you feel the frustration of having so much to do. You're working with products that are staples for the American consumer, so the company's commitment to quality is very important.

I usually start work at seven-thirty in the morning—the company hours are eight to four-thirty—and leave between six-thirty and seven-thirty at night. Most days are so busy that the only time you can work without interruptions is before and after normal working hours. Occasionally I take work home in the evenings, and one or two weekends a month I spend a few hours at home writing memos or getting through my mail. You do what you have to do to get the job done.

I think my job is fascinating. The most frustrating part is a lack of knowledge at times. There are so many things I want to know but I can't possibly understand right away. But I wouldn't want a job where I didn't learn something every day. As you move up, this increased knowledge allows you to make decisions with greater impact.

REAL ESTATE

t wasn't too long ago that the real estate industry primarily attracted part-time workers like homemakers and retirees who wanted flexible hours and the opportunity to make a little extra money. For most parts of the United States, those days are long gone. Many college graduates have decided to make their careers in the buying and selling of commercial and residential property. In addition to bringing together buyers and sellers of property, real estate professionals are increasingly involved in more complex activities, such as running sophisticated development and leasing enterprises, managing property holdings for clients, and appraising commercial property.

Part of the reason that the real estate trade has evolved from a part-time endeavor to full-time occupation is the growth of national real estate companies. In the past, real estate typically was a local business; independent agents generally focused on a few towns or counties in a state and had no need to expand their operations. The growth of nationwide companies like Century 21 and Coldwell Banker did much to change the face of the real estate profession. The fact that real estate values have soared in most areas of the nation over the last two decades also changed the business dramatically. The simple fact is that there is too much money to be made in real estate to be ignored.

Like the stock market, the real estate market is subject to ups and downs, although conventional wisdom rightly holds that investments in property are sounder than investments in paper. In the late 1970's and early 1980's, few regions were as hot as the Southwest, particularly the Houston area. Soaring oil prices created an economic boom there, and businesses flocked to the Sun Belt to be close to the action. When the bottom dropped out of the oil market in the mid-1980's, the real estate market sunk as well. Builders who had rushed to put up one office building after the other found themselves holding a lot of empty space. Owners of apartment buildings dangled such incentives as free rent to lure tenants. As the oil market rebounds, however, the real estate business should also get brighter in that region.

Job seekers in the real estate business will find opportunities in the following areas:

◆ RESIDENTIAL AND COMMERCIAL SALES

◆ APPRAISAL

◆ PROPERTY MANAGEMENT

Although residential real estate transactions are by far more numerous, commercial transactions usually are more lucrative. The arithmetic is simple: an agent who sells seven $200,000 homes won't make as much commission as one who makes a $2 million commercial property sale. In some areas of the country, New York, Boston, San Francisco, and Los Angeles among them, commissions of $500,000 or more for commercial deals are not unheard of. Of course, few agents will ever have a chance at the real big deal; but stringing a healthy number of smaller deals together can be just as rewarding.

Computer technology will continue to revolutionize the real estate business. As image processing systems become a reality, agents will be able to "show" prospective buyers properties just by accessing files on a computer screen. Such technology certainly will cut down on the amount of time that agents spend bringing customers to properties that turn out to be wholly unsuitable. It will also enable offices in different regions to share their listings more easily. For instance, a commercial buyer in New England who's interested in opening a facility in Georgia won't have to make countless trips to view and evaluate available sites.

If you want to become a broker, the type of degree you've earned isn't as important as your initiative and sales ability. Many consider sales the most challenging and lucrative area of real estate. The most successful brokers are people who possess excellent communications skills, an entrepreneurial spirit, and a broker's license. One liability for recent graduates who are considering sales is that you may have to forgo income for as long as six months after you begin working, since most employers do not pay a salary. Earnings are based on commissions from listings and sales.

A bachelor's degree in business or a strong core of business courses is helpful if you plan to go into some of the more technical areas of real estate, such as commercial appraisal or development.

JOB OUTLOOK

JOB OPENINGS WILL GROW: About average

COMPETITION FOR JOBS: Some

Expect the most competition for the more technical jobs, particularly those available at commercial banks.

NEW JOB OPPORTUNITIES: Real estate has become part of the world of high finance. Brokerage firms, most notably Merrill Lynch, have instituted their own real estate affiliates. Property now competes with stocks and bonds as a form of investment. A piece of property bought solely for its investment potential has the same status as a security. The investment is originated (financed), managed, and resold for maximum profit through the process known as syndication. This is a sophisticated area for which an M.B.A. is often a prerequisite. Still, it is possible to acquire the necessary knowledge of this function through sales work.

GEOGRAPHIC JOB INDEX

Employment opportunities exist wherever there are properties—houses, office buildings, stores, farms, factories, retirement developments, and resorts. Commercial real estate firms are most often located in major cities. The dense population and large numbers of businesses in cities creates brisk competition for both residential and commercial sites and consequently a high rate of turnover. A majority of the major finance companies are located in cities as well, facilitating real estate transactions.

WHO THE EMPLOYERS ARE

NATIONAL REAL ESTATE FIRMS AND FRANCHISES usually specialize in either commercial or residential sales, although some of the largest ones handle both. A firm is a single company with agency branches, while a franchise leases its name, training program, and advertising to independent agencies who want to be affiliated with a recognized company. (Century 21 is one of the largest such franchises.) A real estate firm usually hires from a central office, while each local franchise does its own hiring.

LOCAL AND REGIONAL REALTY FIRMS are small, often family-owned agencies that primarily handle residential and small commercial transactions.

APPRAISAL COMPANIES specialize in evaluating the market value of buildings and property, both commercial and residential. They offer fewer jobs than do real estate firms, but are growing in number.

MANAGEMENT FIRMS administer and manage property, primarily commercial property. Many specialize in one type of establishment—apartment buildings, office buildings, resorts, or commercial holdings.

BANKS AND BROKERAGE HOUSES are hiring an increasing number of people to handle appraisals, syndications, and development. They often look for candidates with specific financial skills or with a year or two of experience in some real estate specialty.

MAJOR EMPLOYERS

COMMERCIAL REAL ESTATE FIRMS
Arthur Rubloff & Co., Chicago, IL
Coldwell Banker, Los Angeles, CA
Cushman & Wakefield, New York, NY
Grubb & Ellis, Oakland, CA
Merrill Lynch Realty, New York, NY

RESIDENTIAL REAL ESTATE FIRMS AND FRANCHISES
Beard & Warner, Chicago, IL
Century 21, Irvine, CA
Henry S. Miller, Dallas, TX
Shannon & Luchs, Washington, DC
Van Schaack & Co., Denver, CO

HOW TO BREAK INTO THE FIELD

Very few real estate firms recruit on campus, but it's worth finding out if any plan to visit your school's placement office. Although few universities offer a real estate curriculum, many offer real estate courses through their adult or continuing education divisions. You cannot earn degree credit by taking one or more of these courses, but you often can earn continuing education credits that will help you fulfill the requirements for a sales license. Most states require candidates for the general sales license to complete 40 hours of classroom instruction. You must then take an examination, which includes questions on basic real estate transactions and on laws affecting the sale of property. In addition, there is a state given exam, which must be passed. Some states have license reciprosity and others do not, so make sure to check with your local real estate board.

The best way to identify potential employers in a particular area is to check the Yellow Pages under Residential or Commercial Real Estate. The office or institute that administers the real estate program often has information about local employers.

Most real estate firms require entry-level salespeople to have a sales license or at least to be enrolled in a preparatory program. The best way to land a sales spot is to set up an interview with the manager of a firm. How well you sell yourself in the interview will be the major factor in the decision to hire you as a salesperson.

INTERNATIONAL JOB OPPORTUNITIES

Although some American real estate firms have branches abroad, most of the jobs there would be filled by nationals who have better contacts and knowledge of client needs. Appraisers and developers are the kinds of real estate professionals who are most likely to be called on by foreign businesses to work outside the United States.

ENTREPRENEURIAL

So you want to start your own brokerage firm. Well, join the club. Hundreds of new real estate businesses open every year, and hundreds fail every year. The reasons for failure are many: a sluggish market in a particular region, too much competition from other agencies, an inability to organize an office efficiently, among others.

It takes a lot more than a real estate license to start a successful venture. The first thing that any fledgling venture needs is credibility. Realtors who strike out on their own generally have spent a few years in a specific region, building a solid reputation in the community. A new real estate business also needs the proper conditions for growth. If you're planning on opening the 15th agency in an area that only has room for 10, your chances for success aren't great.

Sometimes, however, an angle on the business can provide the edge that leads to success. In areas of the country where condominium development is on the rise, for instance, some agencies have carved niches for themselves by specializing in condo listings and placements. Others have found profits in relocation, particularly in areas that are undergoing booms in business. Such angles usually aren't strong enough to ensure viability over the long run; but in those critical first years, they can mean the difference between success and failure.

SALES

At one time, an experienced broker would sit a new salesperson down, point to the telephone, and expect results. Success depended largely on personal contacts and bravado. These assets are still a boon, but now they're only the beginning. A successful sale depends on a series of skillfully executed steps.

First you must seek out newly available real estate that is appropriate for the company's listings (e.g., commercial or residential; high-, middle-, or low-income; urban, suburban, or rural). You then follow up by personally inspecting the property. If it is suitable, you must secure the owner's agreement to list with your firm. In the face of competition from other real estate companies that want to list the property, you will have to try to persuade the owner that the property should be listed exclusively with your firm.

Matching clients with listings usually entails many hours of showing properties, getting to know your clients better, and learning how to meet the individual's needs or, in the commercial market, the client company's needs.

In commercial real estate the most important considerations (aside from price, which is always a key factor) are size, location, prestige, and proximity to transportation. Although the client may have very specific requirements in all these areas, a skilled salesperson who understands the market knows how to present worthwhile alternatives. In the residential market individuals also have strong ideas about what type of property they want and how much they can spend, but their final choice often depends on how they feel about the house. A family, for example, may want a house that is near a school, off the main road, and within walking distance of a shopping center. If none of your listings quite fills the bill, it's up to you to spot the client's weakness for, say, southern exposures, fireplaces, and a yard with trees. You may have a property with a strong appeal for the client even though it doesn't satisfy all of the initial criteria.

A new and important aspect of residential sales is relocation management. Some large firms train salespeople to deal with clients who are moving to one area of the country from another. They give clients advice above and beyond the financial aspects of buying a particular property, e.g., which schools or school districts are desirable, what churches, social, and community groups are in the area. In fact, firms specializing in relocation counseling and management are growing in number. Moving can be a traumatic experience for some members of a family, and many relocation firms are headed by psychologists, but they also employ people whose strong point is a good knowledge of the social, cultural, and recreational aspects of the community. The biggest customers of relocation firms are major corporations that are transferring employees from one business location to another.

Some salespeople are better at attracting listings than they are at closing a deal; others have the reverse strengths. As a result, salespeople sometimes put their efforts into one area or the other. If you find that you excel in obtaining listings, don't worry about missing out on sales commissions. It's common practice now for the person obtaining the listing to share in the commission.

QUALIFICATIONS

PERSONAL: Entrepreneurial instincts. Resourcefulness and enthusiasm. Ability to relate to many different types of people. Self-confidence. Perseverance. Good listening skills.

PROFESSIONAL: Sales license. Good math skills. Sales savvy.

CAREER PATHS

LEVEL	JOB TITLE	EXPERIENCE NEEDED
Entry	Salesperson or trainee	Sales experience preferred
2	Broker	College degree a plus, 1–3 years
3	Firm manager or owner	5 + years

JOB RESPONSIBILITIES ♦ ENTRY LEVEL

THE BASICS: Being on floor duty—answering phones, fielding calls for other brokers. Checking newspaper listings for accuracy. In the field, looking for possible properties.

MORE CHALLENGING DUTIES: Showing properties. Doing financial analyses of potential buyers. Negotiating deals between buyers and sellers.

MOVING UP

As a salesperson, you'll be working under the auspices of a broker, whose participation is necessary to close a transaction officially. After you have worked for one to three years (depending on the regulations in your state) and have taken 90 hours of formal training, you'll be eligible to take an exam to become a broker. (If you have a bachelor's degree in real estate, you may be able to get the experience requirement waived.) In sales, the only thing that separates the beginner from the successful broker is experience. The more transactions you're involved in and the more varied the kinds of properties you deal with, the more you'll learn about the business.

APPRAISAL

Appraisers determine market prices for properties ranging from tiny residential plots to vast industrial tracts. Real estate appraisal used to be done primarily by banks, which assessed the worth of a given property when it was being bought or sold by a customer. Offices specializing in this real estate function are sprouting up nationwide, both as independent firms and as divisions of banks. It is becoming a vastly diversified field, involving, in addition to property appraisal, cost analyses for banks, feasibility studies for developers, evaluations of joint ventures between banks, principals and developers, and other related functions.

Appraisers do not need a sales license, but they must take a series of classes and exams to qualify them in different market areas. These are not required for a first job, but appraisers are expected to enroll soon after being hired. Many real estate firms, again, depending on their size, have appraisers on their staffs.

The most significant credential in appraisal is the M.A.I. (Member Appraisal Institute) designation, given by the American Institute of Real Estate Appraisers. Although this credential isn't required, anyone with ambition will pursue it. Only M.A.I. will give you the credibility to go after the most profitable and prestigious accounts. Anywhere from five to ten years of classes and experience are needed to qualify for the exam, at which point you must also produce two demonstration appraisals for evaluation. There are other credentials, too—for example, the S.R.P.A. (senior real property appraiser)—but none of them is as prestigious or as difficult to acquire as the M.A.I.

QUALIFICATIONS

PERSONAL: An eye for detail. A problem-solving mentality. Willingness to make decisions.

PROFESSIONAL: Good writing skills. Analytical ability. Familiarity with specialized real estate markets and trends.

CAREER PATHS

LEVEL	JOB TITLE	EXPERIENCE NEEDED
Entry	Junior appraiser	College degree, business background preferred

2	Appraiser	2–4 years
3	Senior appraiser	5–8 years
4	Partner	8–10 years

JOB RESPONSIBILITIES ♦ ENTRY LEVEL

THE BASICS: Fielding questions from clients. Maintaining files on financial trends and existing accounts.

MORE CHALLENGING DUTIES: Appraising single-family residences. Gathering data (inspecting land deeds and records of transactions that might reflect land value). Doing research and writing reports.

MOVING UP

The longer you're on the job, the more time you can expect to spend doing on-site evaluation, such as appraising "distressed property" values. During your first years you'll be preparing for your M.A.I., which means taking classes and developing a reputation for being a thorough researcher and good judge of property values. Unlike in sales, you can count on more individual attention from the people higher than you, as your work will reflect on them and the company.

PROPERTY MANAGEMENT

As apartment complexes expand, condominiums sprout up, and shopping centers continue to spread in the suburbs and beyond, management of these buildings and units becomes an increasingly important function. Management includes overseeing the physical upkeep of the property, smoothing tenant and community relations, orchestrating rentals and lease renewals, and attending to advertising and the many other duties involved in operating an active property. Although it is not strictly required, most management personnel do possess a sales license, often because they started in sales. However, when management agencies take over the responsibility of leasing properties for their principals, the license becomes crucial.

QUALIFICATIONS

PERSONAL: Problem-solving mentality. Outgoing personality. Ability to work with all types of people. Willingness to take charge.

PROFESSIONAL: Financial background. Administrative skills. Organization skills. Computer know-how. Awareness of local politics.

CAREER PATHS

LEVEL	JOB TITLE	EXPERIENCE NEEDED
Entry	Trainee or administrative assistant	College degree, business background preferred
2	Assistant property manager	3 years
3	Manager	5 years
4	Area property manager	10+ years

JOB RESPONSIBILITIES ♦ ENTRY LEVEL

THE BASICS: Answering phones. Keeping tenant files. Billing accounts.

MORE CHALLENGING DUTIES: Inspecting building upkeep. Arranging for repairs. Keeping in close contact with the building superintendent. Attending meetings with tenants. Working with community officials—police, sanitation, and other departments.

MOVING UP

As you gain more experience, you might become involved in making reports on buildings in order to have them certified or recertified for government subsidies. You will begin to take on responsibilities from the office management—dealing with contractors or subcontractors hired to do particular repairs. The ability to handle a number of projects simultaneously and to satisfy the demands of many different people will stand you in good stead in your quest for more responsible positions.

ADDITIONAL INFORMATION

SALARIES

SALES

Sales earnings are almost invariably in the form of commissions. Generally speaking, the firm gets 6 percent of the sale price, paid when a residential deal is closed. Of this, the broker gets half. In commercial work, the terms of a sales agreement vary, depending on how many principals are involved, whether the agent is handling the property management, the intended use of the building (i.e., development, upgrade and resale, or commercial leasing), and other considerations. Consequently, the commerical broker must be skilled at predicting and weighing the many factors that affect a sale.

When you begin you can expect an annual income in the low to mid-twenties after your initial startup period. Commercial sales will bring you quickly into a high-income bracket.

Many commercial brokers make more than $100,000 a year and few make less than $50,000. Residential sales will yield a more moderate income unless your properties are very expensive.

APPRAISAL

In commerical appraisal, you'll start out in the low to mid-twenties annually, but after several successful years you will probably earn $30,000 to $40,000 per year. Senior appraisers can make $100,000 and more a year, if they're ambitious and their firms transact deals of significant size. Salaries are lower for those who go into residential appraisal.

PROPERTY MANAGEMENT

Entry-level salaries start in the teens to low-twenties, but with several year's experience, your yearly salary can be in the $30,000 to $40,000 range.

WORKING CONDITIONS

SALES

HOURS: Your schedule will vary greatly from day to day because properties are shown during clients' free time. That often means you're on the job after five o'clock and on weekends. Many offices rotate floor duty among sales staff, who sign up for or are assigned shifts during regular office hours at least once, and sometimes several times, a week.

ENVIRONMENT: In commercial real estate you'll probably find yourself in comfortable office surroundings, with computers beeping, phones ringing, and typewriters clacking. To start, you will probably share an office with one or more people on the sales staff.

In residential sales, offices are attractive and are often located in a converted house, frequently one representative of the kinds of properties that the firm deals in. Condominium brokers frequently use one of their units as an on-site sales office until all the rest are filled. Firms also set up offices in shopping centers and business areas.

WORKSTYLE: Count on a lively pace and lots of variety, at least in the periods when business is brisk. You might be out canvassing new sites or showing old ones. You might be on the phone answering queries or taking property profiles. At night, you could be closing a sale over dinner or taking classes.

TRAVEL: You can expect to travel a lot in your immediate locality, but not much farther. Firms that take part in, or run, national referral services generally depend on the service to take care of business generated in distant places. Usually only the firm's officers and the more experienced company members attend realtors' conventions in other cities.

APPRAISAL

HOURS: In the beginning, you will not be working much more than 40 hours a week. As you take on more responsibility and see projects through, you'll be coming in early, staying late, and working weekends.

ENVIRONMENT: Most appraisal offices are located in business districts in metropolitan areas. Officers will be comfortable and, without a doubt, computerized. To start, you'll share office space with others at the same general level.

WORKSTYLE: Your time will be more or less equally divided among doing evaluations at property sites, researching records in government offices, and preparing reports and analyses in your own office.

TRAVEL: Somewhat more opportunity for travel exists here than in sales. Contracts are often made with developers, builders, and investors in other parts of the country, where a large amount of on-site time will be required. An appraiser's jobs may include travel overseas, but rarely at entry level.

PROPERTY MANAGEMENT

HOURS: Hours are usually nine to five, unless you must stay late to inspect a repair job or attend a tenant meeting.

ENVIRONMENT: Offices are hectic, since many people are involved in management, all with varying concerns and responsibilities.

WORKSTYLE: You may spend as much time out of the office as in it during your first year, checking boilers for heat efficiency, monitoring tenant association meetings, or persuading local politicians to increase police protection at a shopping center. This is in addition to your share of office duties.

TRAVEL: There's virtually no travel, since the property you manage will be in the vicinity of your office.

EXTRACURRICULAR ACTIVITIES/WORK EXPERIENCE

College yearbook, newspaper, other campus publications—selling ad space
Campus fund-raising events—serving as a student adviser or helping with placement, working as a caretaker or superintendent
Campus dormitories—working as a resident adviser

INTERNSHIPS

Because there are virtually no formal internships in the real estate industry, the best way to obtain experience is to contact a local real estate firm and apply for work during their busy season.

RECOMMENDED READING

BOOKS
Handbook for Real Estate Market Analysis by John M. Clapp, Prentice-Hall: 1987

How to Master the Art of Selling Real Estate, Judy Slack ed., Tom Hopkins International Inc.: 1988

How to Teach Real Estate to Adults, Real Estate Educators Association: 1989

Real Estate Finance, by Sherman J. Maisel, Harcourt Brace Jovanovich: 1987

Your Successful Real Estate Career by Kenneth W. Edwards: 1987

PERIODICALS
Journal of Real Estate Education (quarterly), National Association of Realtors, 430 North Michigan Avenue, Chicago, IL 60611

National Real Estate Investor (monthly), 6255 Barfield Road, N.E., Atlanta, GA 30328

Real Estate Business and Investment Journal, National Association of Realtors, 430 N. Michigan Avenue, Chicago, IL 60611

Real Estate Education Journal (annual), Real Estate Educator's Association, 230 N. Michigan Avenue, Chicago, IL 60601

Real Estate Forum (monthly), 12 West 37th Street, New York, NY 10018

Real Estate Weekly (weekly), Hagendorn Communications, 1 Madison Avenue, New York, NY 10011

PROFESSIONAL ASSOCIATIONS

The largest professional association is the National Association of Realtors (NAR), headquartered in Washington, DC, and Chicago, IL. It has eight major branches of operations:

American Chapter of International Real Estate Federation
American Institute of Real Estate Appraisers
American Society of Real Estate Councilors
Institute of Real Estate Management
Real Estate Securities & Syndication Institute
Realtors National Marketing Institute
Society of Industrial Realtors
Women's Council of Realtors

All have chapters or branch offices around the country. Most offer classes that are open to the public for fees ranging from $400 to $800. These are intensive daytime classes lasting from one to two weeks. Many local institutes are affiliated with the NAR, which exerts a strong influence on the field. Send queries to either of their two headquarters:

National Association of Realtors
430 North Michigan Avenue
Chicago, IL 60611

National Association of Realtors
777 Fourteenth Street, N.W.
Washington, DC 20005

Check your city or state university to see if they offer the Real Estate Salesperson's course.

INTERVIEWS

RICHARD MARCHITELLI
PARTNER
MARCHITELLI & KING ASSOCIATES

I graduated in 1969 with a B.A. in political science from Belmont Abbey College, Belmont, North Carolina. I had always planned to attend law school. During college vacations, I worked in a real estate appraisal office doing research. I began to write portions of reports and was permitted to perform simple analytical tasks, and my interest in real estate appraising and consulting began to grow. Nevertheless, upon graduation from college I entered law school.

The more I became interested in appraising, the more I became disenchanted with law, so I left after one semester and worked full time for the appraisal company where I was employed during my vacations.

In 1973 I became one of two partners in the company where I was working. By 1975 my partner, who was much older than I, was preparing to retire. I felt that I was at a crossroads in my career and that in order to develop and grow professionally, perhaps I should join a national company. After much soul-searching and a series of interviews, I decided to stay in business for myself and took complete control of the company on the retirement of my partner.

At about this time, I decided to seriously pursue the M.A.I. designation, which I was awarded after fulfilling the demanding requirements. The M.A.I. designation has been invaluable on a business and a professional level. It gives me credibility in the marketplace. It indicates to our clients and other readers of my reports that I have achieved a level of competence that only 3 percent of practicing real estate appraisers have.

On the personel level, I have become very involved in the American Institute of Real Estate Appraisers, working on various local (i.e., chapter) and national committees. I meet regularly with real estate consultants from all over the country, exchanging ideas and viewpoints.

Currently I am serving the AIREA as vice chairman of the national publications committee, which is responsible for publication of all Institute textbooks. In this capacity, I also served as chairman of a special subcommittee that compiled and edited *The Dictionary of Real Estate Appraisal*. I was recently appointed to be 1985 chairman of the publications committee.

In 1982 Edward A. King, Jr. became a partner and principal in this company. The company formally changed its name to Marchitelli King & Associates, Inc. the following year. Currently we employ more than 17 persons.

The business itself is a demanding one. An appraiser must keep abreast of new theories and teachings by reading various professional journals and by regularly attending seminars and courses. Most important are the clients' demands, which center on service and competency.

Real estate consulting is also a pressure business. The inability to meet a deadline could result in the loss of millions or tens of millions of dollars to a client. Often many people are waiting for delivery of one of our reports, which could be used to assist in a lending decision, determine the economic feasibility of a project, aid in the disposition of sale of a property, advise on conversion to an alternate use, and other matters.

Much of my time is spent developing new business, keeping in contact with existing clients, and running the company. An increasing amount of my time is spent as a corporate manager and less as an appraiser. In fact, there are few assignments that I complete totally on my own anymore. My time is also spent reviewing a staff member's work. Actually, 99 percent of the commercial reports leaving the office are still personally reviewed by both my partner and myself.

Managing the business as a business has presented an additional challenge. My partner and I meet monthly to review the company's performance, monitor where recent business has come from, plan development of new business, and discuss where there might be a "window" in the market for our services, offering further diversified services. We also meet weekly with our office manager to discuss performance of the office.

At these meetings we review computer printouts of a program specifically designed to show how much business the company did the previous week, new business that came in, and the performance of individual staff members, in terms of workload, billings, and other areas.

My partner and I still complete special assignments in conjunction with one another or in combination with one or more staff members. Some recent such assignments include the valuation of the leased fee estate underlying the Stanhope Hotel on Fifth Avenue and 81st Street in Manhattan, appraisal of a 2200-acre tract of land with more than ten miles of coastline, preparation of a comparative tax study of industrial properties, a cost benefit study involving a luxury condominium project in New Orleans, and analysis of a joint venture opportunity for a bank consisting of a multiuse building (i.e., residential cooperative apartments, retail condominiums, and office condominiums).

My days are full and busy. They begin at 7 A.M. at the office and often end after 11 P.M. I often work on Saturdays and, once in a while, on Sundays. In addition to the constant pressure, they are filled with luncheon and dinner meetings, staff meetings, corporate business, and telephone calls.

I have been a contributor to professional journals in the past, for example, *The Appraisal Journal*, published by the AIREA. I am also planning to write articles on the real rate of return, valuing cooperative apartment buildings, and deflationary economic pressures on real estate values.

I find the field of real estate appraising/consulting to be challenging and intellectually satisfying. Every day is different. There are always problems requiring new solutions. I could not imagine myself feeling as fulfilled as I do practicing law or doing anything else. I do not merely enjoy this business, I love it.

Real estate appraising can also be financially rewarding. A person with intermediate experience can earn from $35,000 to $50,000 a year. Senior people earn in excess of $100,000 annually.

BETH SIRULL
ACQUISITIONS ASSOCIATE
BOSTON EQUITY INVESTMENTS, INC.
BOSTON, MA

I got my job by answering an ad in the paper, which is highly unusual. The job was a research position in a real estate consulting firm. Now, I knew nothing about property. I majored in political science with a minor in women's studies, but I demonstrated research and writing skills. In fact, I had to submit a writing sample to get this job. I had worked in fund-raising for the development office at Brandeis University and I had researched potential donors.

I took those research skills that I had developed, plus my academic research skills, and applied them to this job in a real estate firm that did studies on potential property development. They taught me everything I know now about the real estate market. But my background is not so unusual. All the people in my firm have liberal arts degrees. The woman who runs my department has a degree in Latin and Greek history.

I try to acquire property for the firm to put investors in. We try to negotiate an agreement with the developer who has a specific type of property. We are only interested in certain types of property. We get an agreement from the developer, package an investment in that property, and turn around and sell it to investors who give us the money to complete the acquisition. I go out and locate property that meets our specifications. I evaluate it, price it, and investigate the market. I ascertain what the developer wants and then try to negotiate an agreement with him. We end up with a contract to do business.

A typical day for me involves some time on the phone and some time on the computer. I have to do a lot of writing because I draft the contracts. I also send out marketing letters to people. It depends on what phase we are in. I spend some days on the road and other days are spent entirely on the phone.

I love when I am out on the road and looking at property. I like to talk to developers. I do, on the other hand, have to spend a lot of time making cold phone calls trying to find a developer who has what we want. I don't like this very much. It is almost like sales. It's like finding a needle in a haystack sometimes. Another way to look at what I do, besides acquiring property, is that my company provides a financial service to a developer. We provide financing for his project. I'm really marketing a service. The developer needs money and I want us to be the provider and not one of our competitors.

A person who wants to work in real estate needs the basic skills that an industry is looking for. You have to be able to speak and write well. You have to be able to determine not only answers, but you have to know what questions to ask. You have to know where information is and how to get it. This is especially true for phone research. These are all the skills you learn in college and I think that a liberal arts degree really is worthwhile for this career.

If you are just out of college and you want to go into real estate I would advise you to get whatever entry level job you can find. Also, be willing to work for very little money in the beginning. In the long haul you can make a good living. In the beginning the most important thing is to just get the experience. Learn to live on what you make. I barely ate on my first job's salary, but I stuck with it and it's paying off in the long run.

BIBLIOGRAPHY

The American Almanac of Jobs and Salaries, by John W. Wright, Avon Publishers: revised annually

Careers in Education, by Roy A. Edelfelt, VGM Career Horizons: 1988

College Placement Annual, by the College Placement Council: revised annually (available in most campus placement offices)

Directory of Department Stores and Mail Order Firms, by the editors of Chain Store Guide, Lebhar Friedman Inc.: revised periodically

Encyclopedia of Careers and Vocational Guidance, Vol. II; Selecting a Career, J. G. Ferguson Publishing Co.: 1984

Handbook for Real Estate Market Analysis, by John M. Clapp, Prentice-Hall Inc.: 1987

Jobs! Where They Are . . . What They Are . . . What They Pay, by Robert O. Snelling and Anne M. Snelling, Simon and Schuster: 1985

National Directory of Addresses and Telephone Numbers, Concord Reference Books: revised annually

National Survey of Occupational Social Workers, by Robert J. Teare, National Association of Social Workers: 1987

Occupational Outlook Handbook, U.S. Department of Labor Bureau of Statistics: revised annually

Opportunities in Personnel Management, by William J. Traynor, National Textbook Inc.: 1983

A Profession at Risk, by Terry Dozier, Education Commission of the States: 1986

Professional Choices: Values at Work, by Ann A. Abbott, National Association of Social Workers: 1988

What Color Is Your Parachute? A Practical Manual for Job Hunters and Career Changers, by Richard N. Bolles, Ten Speed Press: revised periodically

SALES

Every product you use or see has got a sales force behind it, whether it's the toothpaste you use before going to bed, or the car you'll drive to work. If you were the type of person who set up the lemonade stands on these steamy summer days or had the most successful paper route in your town, sales could be the area for you. While it can take some time to work up the ladder, the payoffs can be quite handsome. Some sales people make more from commissions than the salaries of the top executives in their companies. Sales also allows people to jump from one industry to another. The fundamentals of good selling don't change from industry to industry, although adjustments do have to be made.

In this section, we profile the sales of seven different industries. These seven can be grouped into three larger categories: **advertising media sales,** including magazines, radio, and newspapers; **business and financial services,** including real estate, insurance, and securities; and **manufactured products,** which includes all products from pharmaceuticals to clothes to cars. People wanting to break into sales will do best first to decide which one of these three areas they are most interested in and then choose a specific industry to pursue.

ADVERTISING SPACE SALES

Because most newspapers rely on advertising revenue rather than subscriptions or single copy sales for financial viability, a hardworking, creative sales department is a must. A successful salesperson first has to convince a potential client that the newspaper will provide his or her product with the widest possible exposure to the right audience.

Newspaper advertisements fall into two categories: display and classified. Display ads, found throughout the newspaper, are often illustrated and can cover an entire page or spread. The classified section advertises help wanted, merchandise for sale, real estate, etc. It's often easier to land an entry-level position in classified ad sales than in display sales, especially on a major metropolitan daily.

As competition for advertising dollars has become keener, the space sales department has had to become more organized and "scientific" in the way it conducts business. Because more and more newspapers are requiring applicants to have a college degree and sales know-how to land a job in space sales, it is rapidly becoming an attractive opportunity for highly motivated, personable, and energetic graduates.

QUALIFICATIONS

PERSONAL: An outgoing personality. Resourcefulness. Initiative. Persistence.

PROFESSIONAL: Good phone manner. Typing. Written and oral communications skills. Understanding of advertising techinques. Familiarity with or sales experience in an industry that advertises in print, particularly the retail business.

CAREER PATHS

LEVEL	JOB TITLE	EXPERIENCE NEEDED
Entry	Account executive (display) or telemarketing sales representative (classified), small- or medium-size newspaper	College degree

	Account executive (display) or telemarketing sales experience representative (classified), major metropolitan newspaper	1–2 years' sales
2	Advertising manager, small- or medium-size newspaper	4–6 years
	Advertising manager, major metropolitan newspaper	7–10 years
3	Advertising director (display or classified), small- or medium-size newspaper	10 years
	Advertising director (display or classified), major metropolitan newspaper	15+ years

JOB RESPONSIBILITIES ♦ ENTRY LEVEL

THE BASICS: In classified ad sales: taking orders over the phone or from walk-in customers. In display: assisting experienced sales personnel. Helping with correspondence, phone calls, and other detail work.

MORE CHALLENGING DUTIES: Soliciting the business of small clients with phone calls and visits. Making sure that ads appear in the right space at the right time.

MOVING UP

Your progress will be measured in easily definable terms: how many advertising dollars you bring in. The more small accounts you handle successfully, the more freedom you'll have in developing new business and the more major accounts you'll be given. Unlike other types of jobs, the nature of your responsibilities won't change dramatically, but as you move up you'll be dealing with more prestigious accounts and will find higher-ranking people as your client contacts. You may, however, begin specializing in a certain category of client—retail, automotive sales, employment agencies, particularly if you work for a major metropolitan paper with a large sales staff. Specialization allows you to develop a broad understanding of your client's needs, to service the account better, and persuade the client to increase the amount of advertising he or she buys from your paper. The most experienced account executives handle national advertisers.

RADIO SALES

As a salesperson or account executive, you'll be selling air time—a precious commodity. And if you're good at it, sales is the quickest path to station management. As a roving representative of your station, you'll get to know your town as well as the mayor knows it, and you'll have the opportunity to meet and eat with the prime movers and shakers. There's no place for introverts or clock-watchers, and the competition to sell air time can be fierce.

You'll have plenty of "studying" to do before you can go out and break sales records. You'll need to "learn your numbers," starting with the rate card, which lists the rates advertisers must pay for air time, and the ratings, which measure the size of the listening audience, so that you can tell a prospective advertiser what a commercial of any length at any time of day would cost. Your station may not be top-ranked in its area, but it may cater to a particular group, which is a strong selling point.

To land the business of a new advertiser, you'll have to give a formal presentation to your prospect. This represents long hours of work over a period of several weeks in which you learn all there is to know about the prospect's needs and marketing plans, his or her customer's buying patterns, and the pros and cons of the products or services to be advertised. You present your findings in the form of an attractive booklet, often accompanied by a sample commercial on a cassette. Building air time sales is critical to your station's success—and your own.

QUALIFICATIONS

PERSONAL: An outgoing personality. Great powers of persuasion. Energy, drive, and persistence.

PROFESSIONAL: Good organizational skills. A facility with numbers. Basic understanding of business concepts. Good typing skills (45 words per minute or better). A pleasant phone manner.

CAREER PATHS

LEVEL	JOB TITLE	EXPERIENCE NEEDED
Entry	Sales assistant/sales trainee	College degree
2	Account executive	1–3 years
3	Sales manager	3–7 years
4	Station manager	10–15 years

JOB RESPONSIBILITIES ♦ ENTRY LEVEL

THE BASICS: Answering phones. Typing letters and sales presentations. Photocopying and filing. Light computer work, e.g., typing into a terminal linked to the traffic department to get scheduling information for clients.

MORE CHALLENGING DUTIES: Accompanying account excecutives on sales calls. Handling a few small accounts on your own. Generating new accounts by writing letters and making phone calls.

MOVING UP

As an account executive, you'll be given a quota and a list of prospects whom you are expected to transform into active clients. You're expected to add new names to the list and increase the advertising orders of existing clients.

If you're a salesperson who shows administrative ability, you may eventually be in line for the position of assistant sales manager, or even sales manager. In addition to servicing your own clients, you'll assist the newer account executives with theirs—overseeing sales contracts, approving scheduling, pointing out prospects, listening to problems, explaining policy, and encouraging stronger sales efforts.

A solid record of success as general sales manager could land you the general manager's job. The general manager sets and implements station policy, handles the station's relations with the FCC and other government agencies, and participates in many community activities on behalf of the station.

SECURITIES SALES

Brokers (also known as account executives, registered representatives, or salespeople) act as agents for people buying or selling securities. Because the performance of an account executive is crucial to the client's satisfaction and the firm's reputation, candidates are put through a rugged qualifying process at any large brokerage firm. The first hurdle is usually a general aptitude test; if you complete that successfully, you'll be interviewed by a succession of people, usually beginning with a corporate recruiter or a branch manager, who will rate your potential for success as a broker. The final hurdle will be a measurement of your sales skills in a test that includes exercises simulating problems and situations commonly faced by brokers. These involve telephone calls to prospects and relevant analytical work. Try to talk to a broker beforehand to prepare for this phase of the process.

As a beginning broker, your aim will be to build up a clientele. The best place to start is with people you know—family, friends, neighbors, members of groups or clubs to which you belong. You'll also be combing phone directories and mailing lists for names of prospective clients and spending the bulk of each day soliciting (many firms expect new brokers to make between 50 and 100 phone calls a day). While you continue to search for new business you'll be servicing your clients: keeping them abreast of their stocks' performance, executing trades, and recommending financial investments suitable to their needs and objectives.

Brokers usually specialize in one type of security, either stocks or bonds, and also either in retail sales, where your clients are individuals, or institutional sales. In addition, there are floor brokers, who work on the floor of a stock exchange, executing the actual trades of listed stocks.

To become a broker, you must pass the licensing exam given by the New York Stock Exchange, the main regulatory body for all the exchanges. In order to take the test, you must be sponsored by a firm. The firm that hires you will put you through an intensive account executive training program and give you study guides to help you prepare for the licensing exam. During the first three months of your training, while you prepare for the exam, you'll be observing the activities of a working brokerage firm. An additional month might be spent taking courses at the firm's training center.

During the next year, you'll be a broker-in-training at a branch office, with the manager of the branch serving as your supervisor. While you're in training, you'll be paid a salary. Once the training period ends you'll be working strictly on commission, so your income will depend on how many transactions you process. Because brokerage firms demand a high level of productivity (many expect to see brokers earn about $50,000 in gross commission the first year), be prepared to work hard.

QUALIFICATIONS

PERSONAL: Self-confidence. Personality. Foresight. Drive. Persistence. Ability to influence others. The strength to withstand frequent rejection.

PROFESSIONAL: Ability to work comfortably with numbers. Understanding of basic business concepts. Previous sales experience preferred.

CAREER PATHS

LEVEL	JOB TITLE	EXPERIENCE NEEDED
Entry	Sales trainee	College degree, sales experience helpful
2	Account executive	1–3 years
3	Branch manager	4–6 years
4	Regional manager	6–10 years
5	National sales manager	10+ years

JOB RESPONSIBILITIES ♦ ENTRY LEVEL

THE BASICS: Identifying prospective clients through mailing lists, phone directories, and making cold telephone solicitations. Answering client's telephone queries. Reading financial publications. Processing transactions.

MORE CHALLENGING DUTIES: Advising clients on appropriate investment strategies. Keeping current clients informed of their stocks' performance by telephone or letter. Studying reports from the research department.

MOVING UP

Your success depends on how hard you're willing to work. The number and quality of clients you can attract, your investment acumen, the soundness of the judgments you make on the basis of factual material from the research department, and your willingness to do more than simply take orders from your clients. It takes years to build a reputation as a broker who knows his or her business thoroughly. If you become a top performer in your branch and have managerial know-how, you may be offered the job of branch manager.

If you reach that point, you'll be required to relinquish all but a few of your clients. (You may be able to retain those with whom you have a personal relationship or who are your biggest investors.) As a branch manager, you'll be paid a salary plus a bonus based on the amount of money the branch office brings in. In addition, you will collect commissions on any transactions you continue to make.

INSURANCE SALES

Sales agents are the backbone of the industry. They're responsible for helping to plan their clients' financial security. In addition to bringing new business to the company, they often help clients file claims and keep them informed about new or better insurance options. They are also responsible for encouraging the client to renew his or her policy.

The two types of agents are those who work on contract for a small salary, benefits, and commissions for one company, and those who work exclusively on commission for many different insurance companies. The latter are often referred to as brokers or independent agents.

According to the Bureau of Labor Statistics, approximately one of every four agents is self-employed. Some agents specialize in either health/life or casualty/property. Others sell both types of insurance. It is not uncommon for the independent agent to sell real estate or to advise on special financial options, such as annuities or mutual funds, in addition to selling insurance policies.

Agents must be licensed in the state where they sell insurance. Licensing usually requires that the individuals pass a state examination that tests knowledge of insurance principles and state insurance laws.

QUALIFICATIONS

PERSONAL: Drive. Willingness to work hard to develop a clientele. Good appearance. Self-assurance. Friendly, outgoing, not easily discouraged.

PROFESSIONAL: Excellent oral communications skills. Ability to make sales presentations. Understanding of the personal and financial needs of diverse groups of people.

CAREER PATHS

LEVEL	JOB TITLE	EXPERIENCE NEEDED
Entry	Sales trainee, sales representative	High school diploma; college degree helpful
2	Sales agent	6–18 months
3	Sales manager	3–5 years
4	District manager	5–7 years
5	Regional manager	7–10 years
6	Vice president, sales	10+ years

JOB RESPONSIBILITIES ♦ ENTRY LEVEL

THE BASICS: Learning about the business of selling insurance. Attending sales strategy sessions as an observer or "tailing" an experienced agent on his or her calls. Assisting established agents to service accounts.

MORE CHALLENGING DUTIES: Making sales calls. Servicing new accounts. Finding and soliciting potential clients.

MOVING UP

Successful salespeople often rise quickly in the insurance business. Sales careers can lead to positions as regional, district, and general managers, as well as corporate vice presidencies. In order to move up you must not only show creativity and ability in selling and servicing your accounts, you must also demonstrate your potential as a manager. To move into the corporate structure you must acquire a broad understanding of all functions of the company and of the insurance industry in general.

REAL ESTATE SALES

At one time, an experienced broker would sit a new salesperson down, point to the telephone, and expect results. Success depended largely on personal contacts and bravado. These assets are still a boon, but now they're only the beginning. A successful sale depends on a series of skillfully executed steps.

First you must seek out newly available real estate that is appropriate for the company's listings (e.g., commercial or residential; high-, middle-, or low-income; urban, suburban, or rural). You then follow up by personally inspecting the property. If it is suitable, you must secure the owner's agreement to list with your firm. In the face of competition from other real estate companies that want to list the property, you will have to try to persuade the owner that the property should be listed exclusively with your firm.

Matching clients with listings usually entails many hours of showing properties, getting to know your clients better, and learning how to meet the individual's needs. In the commercial market the client company's needs must be met.

In commercial real estate the most important considerations aside from price, which is always a key factor, are size, location, prestige, and proximity to transportation. Although the client may have very specific requirements in all these areas, a skilled salesperson who understands the market knows how to present worthwhile alternatives. In the residential market individuals also have strong ideas about what type of property they want and how much they can spend, but their final choice often depends on how they feel about the house. A family, for example, may want a house that is near a school, off the main road, and within walking distance of a shopping center. If none of your listings quite fills the bill, it's up to you to spot the client's weakness for southern exposures, fireplaces, and a yard with trees. You may have a property with a stong appeal for the client even though it doesn't satisfy all of the initial criteria.

A new and important aspect of residential sales is relocation management. Some large firms train salespeople to deal with clients who are moving to one area of the country from another. They give clients advice above and beyond the financial aspects of buying a particular property, e.g., which schools or school districts are desirable, what churches, social, and community groups are in the area. In fact, firms specializing in relocation counseling and management are growing in number. Moving can be a traumatic experience for some members of a family, and many relocation firms are headed by psychologists, but they also employ people whose strong point is a good knowledge of the social, cultural, and recreational aspects of the community. The biggest customers of relocation firms are major corporations that are transferring employees from one business location to another.

Some salespeople are better at attracting listings than they are at closing a deal, others have the reverse strengths. As a result, salespeople sometimes put their efforts into one area or the other. If you find that you excel in obtaining listings, don't worry about missing out on sales commissions. It's common practice now for the person obtaining the listing to share in the commission.

QUALIFICATIONS

PERSONAL: Entrepreneurial instincts. Resourcefulness and enthusiasm. Ability to relate to many different types of people. Self-confidence. Perseverance. Good listening skills.

PROFESSIONAL: Sales license. Good math skills. Sales savvy.

CAREER PATHS

LEVEL	JOB TITLE	EXPERIENCE NEEDED
Entry	Salesperson or trainee	Sales experience preferred
2	Broker	College degree a plus, 1–3 years
3	Firm manager or owner	5+ years

JOB RESPONSIBILITIES ♦ ENTRY LEVEL

THE BASICS: Being on floor duty—answering phones, fielding calls for other brokers. checking newspaper listings for accuracy. In the field, looking for possible properties.

MORE CHALLENGING DUTIES: Showing properties. Doing financial analyses of potential buyers. Negotiating deals between buyers and sellers.

MOVING UP

As a salesperson, you'll be working under the auspices of a broker, whose participation is necessary to close a transaction officially. After you have worked for one to three years (depending on the regulations in your state) and have taken 90 hours of formal training, you'll be eligible to take an exam to become a broker. (If you have a bachelor's degree in real estate, you may be able to get the experience requirement waived.) In sales, the only thing that separates the beginner from the successful broker is experience. The more transactions you're involved in and the more varied the kinds of properties you deal with, the more you'll learn about the business.

MAGAZINE ADVERTISING SALES

Pick up any popular magazine and you can't help noticing the ads. Ads take up as much as half the page space for a very simple reason—ad income provides at least half of the revenue of most magazines.

The job of a magazine sales staff is to sell ad space. Magazine sales people spend much of their time talking to account executives and media planners at ad agencies and at companies whose business they want to cultivate. As a salesperson, you have to convince a potential client that the demographics of your readership match the desired audience. You'll use readership studies and surveys prepared by your magazine and by the industry to prove your point. But you'll also have to research the client's needs by pulling relevant statistics and information from research done about the particular product or service your potential client wants to promote.

The marketing, or sales promotion department, works with sales to develop strategies and provide information that will help the sales staff increase business. The career description below is geared more toward sales because the majority of jobs are there, rather than in marketing or promotion.

The most successful magazines seldom take on beginners in their sales departments. You must first develop a track record at less well-established publications.

QUALIFICATIONS

PERSONAL: Outgoing personality. Good conversationalist. Ability to influence others. Follow through and persistence. Disposition to cope with rejection and not take the word *no* personally.

PROFESSIONAL: Ability to work comfortably with numbers. Understanding of basic business and management concepts. Sales experience preferred for sales jobs. (Note: An increasing number of employers are hiring M.B.A.s for jobs in sales and marketing.)

CAREER PATHS

LEVEL	JOB TITLE	EXPERIENCE NEEDED
Entry	Sales assistant, sales trainee, or secretary	College degree. Sales experience useful
2	Sales representative	1–3 years
3	District or group sales manager	3–7 years
4	Advertising manager	7–10 years
5	Publisher	10–15+ years

JOB RESPONSIBILITIES ♦ ENTRY LEVEL

THE BASICS: Answering telephones. Typing letters. Filing contracts. Sending information to potential clients.

MORE CHALLENGING DUTIES: Writing letters to potential clients. Learning to put together and give presentations. Accompanying more senior people on sales calls. Researching information about prospective clients and their products.

MOVING UP

You must demonstrate the subtle combination of assertiveness and tact that wins advertising dollars. A solid record of successful sales leads to your being assigned larger and tougher accounts. Most of your dealings will be with advertising agencies, which represent individual clients, rather than with the advertisers themselves.

Managers of sales and marketing departments are more concerned with the overall patterns of advertising income and ensuring that the right page space is available for each client. A creative advertising director, who knows the strengths of the publication and can cultivate lasting relationships with dependable advertisers, can make or break a magazine.

MANUFACTURED PRODUCTS

Good salespeople are the fuel that keep any company running. Without them, companies would falter and consumers wouldn't have access to the thousands of products available. In choosing what type of product you might be interested in selling, there are literally thousands of possibilities. It's best to choose an area that you might have some inherent interest in outside of your career. For example, if photography has always been a lifelong hobby, perhaps you'd want to pursue a career selling film and photographic equipment for Kodak. If you've always loved cars and checked out the new models as soon as they came from the assembly plant, perhaps car sales is for you. There are always good opportunities to sell books, especially school or text books. For recent college graduates, it's a path that's particularly rewarding if books have always been a love. There are plenty of other possibilities. Think of the products you like to buy, and you'd probably be pretty good at selling them as well.

It's extremely important for successful sales people to develop trusting relationships with their clients. That means you don't just make a sale to get a commission if it's not something that the client really needs. Next time you try to sell them something, perhaps a new product, they won't be nearly as willing to try it. A salesperson who sells thousands of dollars of kindergarten comic books to a Florida bookstore in a town with only retired people in it has made the sale, and gotten the commission; but next time that person comes in, the buyer's not going to be nearly as willing to go along with the pitch. The most successful sales people are the ones who can identify the client's needs and fill them with their company's products.

Salespeople must keep up with advances in technology. If you sell cameras and you're not aware of the newest type of video camera, for example, your sales and income could drop dramatically. New methods of ordering have also been developed, including the use of faxes and modems; and it's important that sales people stay on top of these developments.

Finally, companies rely on the people in the fiedld for feedback on their new products or on the ones they're testing. Perhaps it's a new type of make-up or the latest designer jacket. Corporate headquarters always likes to hear informed opinions on how products are doing.

QUALIFICATIONS

PERSONAL: Self-starter; friendly; energetic; good phone skills; can take "no" for an answer, and still be enthusiastic.

PROFESSIONAL: Identify a clients need; continual follow-up; build long-term relationships.

CAREER PATHS

LEVEL	JOB TITLE	EXPERIENCE NEEDED
Entry	Sales trainee	High school diploma/ college degree
2	Sales representative	1–2 years
3	Regional sales representative	3–4 years
4	Regional sales manager	6–10 years
5	National sales manager	11–15 years

JOB RESPONSIBILITIES ♦ ENTRY LEVEL

THE BASICS: Take a series of training seminars on personal interaction, getting to know the product, the clients and the territory; paper work developing client list; driving.

MORE CHALLENGING DUTIES: Making sales calls; identifying new customers; identifying needs and filling orders.

MOVING UP

Many of the larger companies have excellent training programs for sales reps. Procter and Gamble's is perhaps the best known for excellent training. Most of the smaller companies won't have any training program at all, but may have you spend a few days on calls with their more experienced reps.

Progress and success in sales is easy to measure: you need only to look at your sales figures from year to year. When they increase significantly you can be assured that the management back at HQ will take note. Often you'll be rewarded with perks, perhaps a trip or free gifts if you exceed your sales quota for the year. After proving yourself for a few years, your move up the ladder will probably come in the form of giving you a new type of product, one that's more popular and perhaps more expensive. This move will, of course, result in a significant increase in income for you.

Many people decide to stop there, keeping the freedom of being a top sales rep and the hefty income. They choose to forego the chance to move to a management position. Other reps who have succeeded in increasing the revenues in their area are then moved to regional managers, responsible not only for their territory but for the reps working under them. The most common division of regions include New England, the Mid-Atlantic, the Southeast, the Central, the South Central, the Mid West, the South West, the North West, and often, California, which is considered a region unto itself.

If you prove successful in managing other reps, then management might decide to bring you into headquarters to handle more advanced sales responsibilities, possibly even the management of all the regional managers in addition to the reps under them. Once you've reached this level, you've really become more of a manager than a sales person.

SECURITIES

Millions of people and institutions in the United States trade in stocks and bonds every day. In fact, many people—those with investments in pension plans and other such benefit programs—have an active interest in the market and don't even know it. Reports on the day's trading, in the guise of the Dow Jones Average and American Exchange ("Amex") averages, are a staple of the daily newspaper and the nightly news broadcast. When the market soars, the nation congratulates itself for its economic health. When it crashes, as it did suddenly and steeply in October 1987, the wounds to the nation's psyche take years to heal.

The business of selling securities is a large and lucrative one. Salaries of a half million dollars a year or more are not unheard of for top analysts and brokers. It's easy to see why so many success-oriented people set their sights on Wall Street—a term that long ago came to stand for the securities industry as a whole.

The term derives from the handsome old beaux arts-style building at 11 Wall Street, a building that is the home of the New York Stock Exchange. The exchange, of course, is not limited to that building. It's linked by hundreds of thousands of miles of communications lines to brokerage offices, and other exchanges around the world. This vast communications network enables a buyer in London, England, for instance, to purchase stock from a seller in California in a matter of minutes.

The thousands of brokerage firms registered with the Securities and Exchange Commission range in size from small, one-office operations to multinational giants like Merrill Lynch. They can be found in cities across the nation and around the world. New York City, however, is the capital of the securities industry, offering more job opportunities than anyplace else.

Although the New York Stock Exchange, or the Big Board, is by far the largest central marketplace in the United States for securities trading, it's not the only one. The American Exchange is located nearby, and there are several regional exchanges: the Pacific, in San Francisco, CA; the Midwest, in Chicago, IL; and others in Boston, MA, Cincinnati, OH, and Philadelphia, PA.

Not every stock can qualify to be listed on one or more of the country's exchanges (requirements for the New York Stock Exchange are the most rigorous). Stocks are traded by brokers who are members of the exchange on which the stock is listed. (A brokerage house may be—and often is—a member of more than one exchange.)

When a broker receives a call from a client who wishes to buy a particular stock, the purchase order is directed to the floor of the appropriate exchange via computer. The brokerage firm has a representative there, called a floor broker. Every listed stock has a trading post, which is a specific location on the exchange's floor, and the floor broker goes there to ask for a quote—both the highest open bid made for the stock and the lowest available offer. Based on the quote, the broker offers a price, shouting out his or her bid for the number of shares the client wants. A floor broker with shares of that stock to sell calls out an offer to sell at the offered price, and a trade is made. The transaction is recorded immediately and the price of the stock is sent back to the broker's office by computer; the broker in turn relays the information to the client. The order is also sent over the wires and appears on the ticker tape in the office of every firm with a seat on that exchange.

Unlisted stocks are traded over the counter. On an electronic visual display unit the broker can call up information listing the securities firms that trade in the various unlisted stocks, and the trade is then conducted directly by telephone.

Securities firms are currently locked in fierce competition with banks for customers' dollars. Recent federal deregulation permits both of these industries to offer products and services that were once the exclusive domain of the other. This means that a broker, in addition to selling stocks and bonds, may now offer clients an array of such products and services as asset management accounts, which pool all a client's assets into a single account. Checks may then be written against the consolidated account. The intense competition between brokers and bankers has resulted in converting many clients who were simple savers into investors.

The computer age has certainly left its mark on the securities industry, although the level of automation is surprisingly low in some areas. On one hand, brokers and analysts have completely automated their operations. They use computers to perform complex computations that take some of the guesswork out of forecasting, provides a host of other services that eliminate much drudgery for researchers, and allows them to expedite client orders. Analysts use microcomputers to analyze balance sheets and cash flow and give brokers fast answers to clients' questions.

The stock exchanges themselves have automated their operations at different paces, a fact that has caused a great deal of market turmoil and controversy. The London stock exchange, for instance, now conducts all its trading via computer terminals. The New York Stock Exchange, meanwhile, runs its trading floor the way it did in the 19th century; traders congregate in "pits" and make trades in person, usually at the tops of their voices.

This clash of old and new came to a head on October 19, 1987. That day, the Dow Jones Industrial Average plummeted by more than 500 points before the head of the NYSE called a halt to trading. In the aftermath of the crash—in which the overall value of stocks declined by over 20 percent—some analysts blamed computers for the severity of the crash. According to these experts, "program trading"—the activation of trades by computer programs based on certain market conditions—caused a market downturn to snowball to near-catastrophic proportions. The events of Black Monday led to the placement of restrictions on program trading, even though some analysts say it was the lack of automation at the NYSE, rather than the use of automation at other exchanges, that caused the crash.

The M.B.A. is highly sought by the securities industry. Although jobs are available to individuals who have only an undergraduate degree, the competition for these positions is fierce and, quite honestly, these people are often overwhelmed by this fast-paced, high-pressured industry. However, your M.B.A. alone will not make you a highly desirable candidate. Employers—especially major firms—like to see relevant work experience, whether in sales or financial research, or some other proof of your ability to succeed.

Jobs are available in the following categories:

◆ **SALES**

◆ **RESEARCH**

◆ **OPERATIONS**

Jobs in the first two areas are most often filled by M.B.A. graduates. Sales work requires the right combination of an outgoing personality, high energy, and excellent judgment; research work requires disciplined analytical abilities.

JOB OUTLOOK

JOB OPENINGS WILL GROW: Faster than average

COMPETITION FOR JOBS: Keen

There are about 15,000 security analysts in the United States, compared with more than 80,000 brokers (and their ranks keep growing), making sales a considerably easier area to crack—assuming you have the required sales experience.

NEW JOB OPPORTUNITIES: The deregulation of the banking industry, the peak performances of the stock market in recent times, and
the dizzying array of new options being made available to investors
are creating new job opportunities in both sales and research.

Deregulation has paved the way for companies to buy up a variety
of financial services and bring them all under one roof to create a
financial supermarket. The first to do so was Sears, Roebuck &
Company. At more than 125 Sears store locations, customers can
now make deposits at Allstate Savings & Loans, purchase insurance
at Allstate Insurance, buy real estate through Coldwell Banker, and
purchase securities through Dean Witter Reynolds.

The fierce competition for investors' money is spurring brokerage
houses to enlarge their sales and research departments to attract
customers, creating more jobs for brokers and analysts.

GEOGRAPHIC JOB INDEX

New York, NY, has the highest concentration of brokerage firms of
any city in the United States, and most of the major firms are
headquartered there, so it's the best place to find jobs in research
and operations. Other cities with a high concentration of brokerage
firms include Boston, MA, Philadelphia, PA, Chicago, IL, Dallas,
TX, San Francisco, CA, and Los Angeles, CA. The major firms
have an extensive network of branch offices (Dean Witter Reynolds,
for example, has more than 325 branch offices throughout the 50
states), and even small cities have one or more brokerage offices. You
could find a job in sales almost anywhere in the country, although
the field is larger, naturally, in a major metropolitan area.

WHO THE EMPLOYERS ARE

NATIONAL BROKERAGE FIRMS employ thousands in their nationwide
branch offices. The biggest of them all, Merrill Lynch, employs
more than 15,000 people. These firms maintain large research
departments and spend millions of dollars tracking down the most
attractive investments for their customers.

REGIONAL BROKERAGE FIRMS provide many of the same services offered by national firms but specialize in trading and promoting the interests of local companies. They employ fewer people than national firms in their offices (all of which are concentrated in their immediate area). Some very small brokerage firms have one office in one city only.

DISCOUNT BROKERAGE HOUSES are firms that do nothing but execute trades. They do not maintain research departments or offer advice, and their fees to investors are correspondingly lower. Many banks are forming partnerships with discount brokers so they can offer their customers discount brokerage services. Two such partnerships are Bank of America and Charles Schwab, and Chase Manhattan Bank and Rose & Company. Many discount brokerage houses are national, but there are local ones as well.

COMMERCIAL BANKS have clients who are principally institutions and individuals with large sums to invest. They employ portfolio managers to handle such investments. Their staffs also include buy-side analysts, who offer purchase recommendations. (Unlike sell-side analysts, who are at securities firms that sell stock, buy-side analysts work for institutions making stock purchases.)

INSURANCE COMPANIES also hire buy-side analysts, who are responsible for advising the company about investing the huge sums of money collected as premiums from policyholders.

MAJOR EMPLOYERS

Merrill Lynch & Co. Inc., New York, NY
Merrill Lynch Pierce Fenner & Smith, New York, NY
Forstmann Little & Co., New York, NY
Shearson Lehman Bros. Holdings, New York, NY
Dean Witter Financial Services, New York, NY
Shearson Lehman Bros. Inc., New York, NY

E.F. Hutton Group Inc., New York, NY
E.F. Hutton & Co. Inc., New York, NY
Prudential Bache Securities, New York, NY
Drexel Burnham Lambert, New York, NY
Paine Webber Group Inc., New York, NY
Drexel B.L. Inc., New York, NY
A.G. Edwards Inc., St. Louis, MO
Kidder Peabody & Co., Inc., New York, NY
Salomon Bros. Inc., New York, NY
Smith Barney Inc., New York, NY

Ranked in order of numbers of employees by Dun's Business Rankings, 1988–89 edition.

HOW TO BREAK INTO THE FIELD

Many securities firms recruit at business schools, but you should not depend only on this source of interviews. The surest route to an interview is through personal contacts. The school's alumni or placement office should be able to direct you to alumni in the industry. If a family member, friend, or neighbor has worked closely with a brokerage firm, don't ignore this possible entree.

If you lack any useful personal contacts, try a letter-writing campaign. If you'd like a job as a broker, write to the account executive recruitment office at the headquarters, or to the branch manager at locations in your area. If your interest lies in operations, write to the operations manager at the firm's headquarters. Send a carefully worded letter stating your qualifications and requesting an interview. Enclose your résumé. Follow it up with a phone call requesting an appointment for an interview.

INTERNATIONAL JOB OPPORTUNITIES

International opportunities are extremely limited. Most of the major firms have offices abroad, but they tend to hire local residents for the positions that exist there.

SALES

Brokers (also known as account executives, registered representatives, or salespeople) act as agents for people buying or selling securities. Because the performance of an account executive is crucial to the client's satisfaction and the firm's reputation, candidates are put through a rugged qualifying process at any large brokerage firm. The first hurdle is usually a general aptitude test. If you complete that successfully, you'll be interviewed by a succession of people, usually beginning with a corporate recruiter or a branch manager, who will rate your potential for success as a broker. The final hurdle will be a measurement of your sales skills in a test that includes exercises simulating problems and situations commonly faced by brokers. These involve telephone calls to prospects and relevant analytical work. Try to talk to a broker beforehand to prepare for this phase of the process.

As a beginning broker, your aim will be to build up a clientele. The best place to start is with people you know—family, friends, neighbors, members of groups or clubs to which you belong. You'll also be combing phone directories and mailing lists for names of prospective clients and spending the bulk of each day soliciting (many firms expect new brokers to make between 50 and 100 phone calls a day). While you continue to search for new business you'll be servicing your clients; keeping them abreast of their stocks' performance, executing trades, and recommending financial investments suitable to their needs and objectives.

Brokers usually specialize in one type of security, either stocks or bonds, and either in retail sales, where clients are individuals, or institutional sales. Another specialized area is that of floor broker, who works on the floor of a stock exchange, executing the actual trades of listed stocks.

To become a broker, you must pass the licensing exam given by the New York Stock Exchange, the main regulatory body for all the exchanges. In order to take the test, you must be sponsored by a firm. The firm that hires you will put you through an intensive account executive training program and give you study guides to help you prepare for the licensing exam. During the first three months of your training, while you prepare for the exam, you'll be observing the activities of a working brokerage firm. An additional month might be spent taking courses at the firm's training center.

During the next year, you'll be a broker-in-training at a branch office, with the manager of the branch serving as your supervisor. While you're in training, you'll be paid a salary. Once the training period ends you'll be working strictly on commission, so your income will depend on how many transactions you process. Since brokerage firms demand a high level of productivity (many expect to see brokers earn about $50,000 in gross commissions the first year), be prepared to work hard.

QUALIFICATIONS

PERSONAL: Self-confidence. Personality. Foresight. Drive. Persistence. Ability to influence others. The strength to withstand frequent rejection.

PROFESSIONAL: Ability to work comfortably with numbers. Understanding of basic business concepts. Previous sales experience preferred.

CAREER PATHS

LEVEL	JOB TITLE	EXPERIENCE NEEDED
Entry	Sales trainee	College degree; sales experience helpful
2	Account executive	1 year
3	Branch manager	3–4 years
4	Regional manager	5–7 years
5	National sales manager	8+ years

JOB RESPONSIBILITIES ♦ ENTRY LEVEL

THE BASICS: Identifying prospective clients through mailing lists and phone directories, and making cold telephone solicitations. Answering clients' telephone queries. Reading financial publications. Processing transactions.

MORE CHALLENGING DUTIES: Advising clients on appropriate investment strategies. Keeping current clients informed of their stocks' performance by telephone or letter. Studying reports from the research department.

MOVING UP

Your success depends on how hard you're willing to work—the number and quality of clients you can attract, your investment acumen, the soundness of the judgments you make on the basis of factual material from the research department, and your willingness to do more than simply take orders from your clients. It takes years to build a reputation as a broker who knows his or her business thoroughly. If you become a top performer in your branch and have managerial know-how, you may be offered the job of branch manager.

If you reach that point, you'll be required to relinquish all but a few of your clients. (You may be able to retain those with whom you have a personal relationship or those who are your biggest investors.) As a branch manager, you'll be paid a salary plus a bonus based on the amount of money the branch office brings in. In addition, you will collect commissions on any transactions you continue to make.

RESEARCH

A broker is only as successful as the company's research department. Knowing which stocks to go after and which to sell comes from listening to the presentations and reading the reports of the firm's researchers, or security analysts, who study stocks and bonds, assess their current value, and forecast their earning potential. Security analysts tend to specialize in a single industry, such as oil or steel, quickly becoming experts in their area.

QUALIFICATIONS

PERSONAL: Ability to work under pressure. Foresight. Self-confidence. Ability to trust your own instincts.

PROFESSIONAL: Verbal and writing skills. Keen analytical skills. Familiarity with accounting procedures. Ability to read between the lines of annual reports. Facility working with a software calc program.

CAREER PATHS

LEVEL	JOB TITLE	EXPERIENCE NEEDED
Entry	Research assistant/junior analyst	College degree
2	Senior analyst	3 + years
3	Managing director	10 years

JOB RESPONSIBILITIES ♦ ENTRY LEVEL

THE BASICS: Reading financial reports. Analyzing corporate balance sheets. Number crunching. Making written recommendations to senior analysts. Assisting senior people at whatever research work needs to be done.

MORE CHALLENGING DUTIES: Accompanying senior analysts on visits to corporation officials to gather firsthand information about the company. Advising the firm's brokers on specific stocks. Fielding questions posed by brokers.

MOVING UP

After a period of gaining familiarity with and expertise in a particular industry, if you demonstrate that your analyses and interpretations of trends and developments are sound, you may be promoted to senior analyst. As a senior analyst, you'll be called on to answer any difficult questions posed by brokers or their clients, and act as adviser on all stocks related to the industry in which you are expert. You'll periodically visit branch offices to deliver oral presentations, accompanied by written reports on your industry to brokers there. You'll also be accompanying institutional salespeople on their visits to lucrative accounts.

OPERATIONS

The operations department, or "back office," is where the hundreds of thousands of daily transactions made by the firm's brokers are processed and recorded. The work is divided among several groups of clerks, each group with specific responsibilities. The purchasing and sales clerks make sure that every buy matches up with a sale by studying the computer printouts that record all transactions. The main source of this information is the Securities Industry Automation Corporation, an automated clearinghouse that is jointly owned by the New York and American Exchanges. The printouts show every buy and sale on these exchanges in a single day; in addition, this same source provides information on national trading. Firms trading on exchanges outside New York, NY, receive comparable information from other automated sources. Clerks in client services post dividends to clients' accounts and mail out monthly statements. Margin clerks keep track of clients' accounts, making sure they haven't purchased more on credit than is legally allowed. Compliance checks ensure that transactions are completed according to all rules and regulations spelled out in the *New York Stock Exchange Constitution and Rules* book. Department heads oversee each of these services.

Securities are received and stored or transferred in a top-security area called the cage, which only a few people in the firm are allowed to enter. Cage clerks microfilm all securities and box them for storage in the vault or transfer them elsewhere to be stored.

An operations supervisor is typically responsible for five to seven clerks, assigning their work, monitoring their productivity, and offering guidance when needed. From supervisor, you may advance to section head; here you act as a liaison between departments and handle day-to-day problems that might prevent the department from functioning smoothly and effectively.

ADDITIONAL INFORMATION

SALARIES

SALES commissions vary with the type of security and the size of the transaction. Retail brokers collect between 30 and 40 percent of the fee that the firm charges for each transaction; institutional brokers collect somewhat less—around 15 percent—because large blocks of securities are being traded. For brokers who bring in a high volume of business, there are numerous incentives, such as free trips and raises in commission. The income potential is unlimited, and some brokers gross in excess of $1 million a year in commissions.

WORKING CONDITIONS

HOURS: A broker's day usually begins at 8 A.M., in time to read the papers and financial journals and talk with the research department before the exchanges open at nine. Brokers often leave the office once trading ends at 4 P.M. Operations work is usually nine to five, with overtime when trading is heavy. Supervisors and section heads put in slightly longer hours, perhaps eight-thirty to six, to catch up with administrative details or attend meetings. Research analysts work the longest hours, typically past 7 P.M.

ENVIRONMENT: Junior brokers, clerks, and junior analysts work in bullpen arrangements. Senior brokers, operations managers, and senior analysts have private offices. Typically, those in sales enjoy the plushest surroundings.

WORKSTYLE: Sales personnel spend a great deal of time on the phone, either speaking with established clients or soliciting new business. Institutional salespeople may wine and dine big clients after normal business hours. Clerks and operations supervisors spend nearly all their time on paperwork, but operations managers may be in meetings up to half of each day. Research is also a desk job; the study of financial statements involves using the microcomputer to arrive at various indicators of a companay's financial status: asset/debt ratio, sales/inventory ratio, sales/debt ratio. You will meet at least once a week with other members of your research team.

TRAVEL: Opportunities to travel are nonexistent for brokers and operations staffs. Regional and national sales managers visit branch offices frequently. As a research analyst, how much you travel and how far you go depends on the industry you cover. If you specialize in an industry the center of which is in your home area, out-of-town trips may be infrequent.

INTERNSHIPS

Many firms are willing to take on M.B.A. students as interns or as temporary employees during summers. You should apply for these positions just as you would for a full-time job. Although some firms announce through campus placement offices that they are looking for interns and temporary help, you should also investigate opportunities on your own.

Because of the growing awareness that on-the-job training is a better test of your abilities than academic experience alone, some large firms are recruiting M.B.A. graduates for intensive, long-term internships that expose them to all areas of the industry. These programs accept candidates on the assumption that these individuals will become full-time employees if they like the industry and can handle the work.

RECOMMENDED READING

BOOKS

Graham and Dodd's Security Analysis by Sidney Cottle, Roger F. Murray, Frank E. Block with collaboration of Martin L. Leibowitz, 5th ed., McGraw-Hill: 1988

Investment and Securities Dictionary by Michael C. Thomsett, Mc-Farland: 1986

Markets: Who Plays, Who Risks, Who Gains, Who Loses by Martin Mayer, Norton: 1988

Moody's International Manual/Moody's Investors Services, The Service: updated regularly

New York Institute of Finance Guide to Investing, The Institute: 1987

Stocks, Bonds, Options, Futures: Investments and Their Markets by the Staff of the New York Institute of Finance, The Institute: 1987

PERIODICALS

Barron's National Business and Financial Weekly (weekly), New York, NY
Business Month (monthly), New York, NY
Business Week (weekly), New York, NY
Changing Times (monthly), Washington, DC
The Economist (weekly), London, England
Entrepreneur (monthly), Los Angeles, CA
Financial World (biweekly), New York, NY
Forbes (biweekly), New York, NY
Fortune (27 times/yr.), New York, NY
Harvard Business Review (monthly), Boston, MA
Inc. (monthly), Boston, MA

Industry Week (every other Monday except in December), Cleveland, OH
Institutional Investor (monthly), New York, NY
Investor's Daily (business days only), Los Angeles, CA
Money (monthly), New York, NY
Nation's Business (monthly), Washington, DC
Personal Investor (bimonthly), Irvine, CA
Savvy (monthly), New York, NY
Sylvia Porter's Personal Finance Magazine (monthly), New York, NY
Success (monthly), New York, NY
Venture (monthly), New York, NY
Wall Street Journal (business days only), New York, NY
Wall Street Transcript (weekly), New York, NY

PROFESSIONAL ASSOCIATIONS

Financial Analyst Federation
1633 Broadway
New York, NY 10019

National Association of Security Dealers
2 World Trade Center
New York, NY 10048

Securities Industry Association
120 Broadway
New York, NY 10271

INTERVIEWS

ASSISTANT VICE PRESIDENT, RESEARCH
L. F. ROTHSCHILD UNTERBERG TOBIN
NEW YORK, NY

I was a triple in college—history, political science, and economics—and I hasten to add that I managed to do that major in economics without taking any courses in mathematics. I definitely did fall into that category of women who have a negative reaction to numbers. Upon graduation I worked for the Corporation for Public Broadcasting in their human resources development. Part of my responsibility was monitoring the employment and portrayal of women and minorities in public broadcasting. That necessitated doing quarterly reports to a congressional committee, and I had to start compiling employment figures, statistics—and there was math staring at me! I later became responsible for the departmental budget, which was rather substantial as our department was responsible for handing out training grants throughout the system. I quickly discovered there was nothing to be frightened about.

I enjoyed that for a while, but got somewhat tired of the nonprofit orientation. It's not very insightful, but the way I ended up in securities was to look in Washington, DC, and to find out what kind of private oriented enterprises there were. There were not many. I won't say "securities" bounced right out of the phone book, but it was the only industry I could see getting into without a great deal of difficulty. I had invested with some success on my own and found it interesting, so I investigated the various brokerage firms in Washington, and found that Ferris and Company, which is a fine regional house in Washington, had a superior, intensive training program.

Once I was in securities I found out that if I wanted to go beyond the basic retail broker status, I had to have a graduate degree. And that's why I went back to school to get an M.B.A. I went to George Washington University while I was still working at Ferris. Because the only management position available at a regional house would be a branch manager, and that certainly was out of the question with my few years of experience, and not having built an enormous clientele book, I decided to come back to New York, which is my native state.

I never liked pure sales and never did cold calling, and quite frankly was uncomfortable with pure commission as a source of income. So I found myself getting more and more involved in the total financial picture of my clients, which gave me a greater level of security in terms of what I was or was not doing with their money. And that was quite suitable experience for the position I now hold in Rothschild's research department. I'm in what's known as portfolio research, and that job entails essentially being a broker to our brokers. They submit their client portfolio with the appropriate investment objective information, and we analyze the portfolio or develop a portfolio to meet the client's needs. The beauty of this is that it gives the client excellent service, because this is done at no additional fee, and I have no vested interest in whether the broker buys or sells. I make decisions on a needs basis for the client versus a need basis for the broker.

The bottom line about having the M.B.A. is that it helped me get the job. I don't know that I use more than 10 percent of what I learned. The program that I was involved in was more qualitative than quantitative, which I frankly liked, and I think an awful lot of large corporations are coming to the conclusion that the quantitative programs are great in the short term, but they're finding that the long-term objectives of many corporations are being sacrificed. That's a consideration one should look at seriously when picking an M.B.A. program. I also think one should work before going for a graduate degree. Although there are hordes of recruiters on campuses these days, and M.B.A.s are still pulling in a fairly nice salary for an initial job, I do think that the allure of the degree without work experience is rapidly dissipating. More and more employers are saying that without experience what you've learned means nothing to you because you haven't been able to apply it while you learned it. The M.B.A. was more a premium degree when I got it than it is today, but it's a question of having the degree to get the door open now.

Sixty to seventy percent of my day is spent talking to brokers, responding to questions on particular stocks about whether they're appropriate for specific clients, looking at portfolios, and going to meetings with other analysts to look at companies or to discuss the general market outlook. The balance of the time is spent with my clients, which is the icing on the cake. I enjoy my salary compensation, and then can do as much commission business as I want. I'm constantly reading research reports of other firms or independent research organizations, and company annual reports, and doing spread sheets on earnings projections. I also function as a conduit between the specialized analysts who cover specific industries and the broker for those securities that our firms covers on a regular basis. When we're talking about companies that are not regularly followed, that's when I have to look at them.

I like the sense of power in this job. It's really rather heady to have brokers who've been on Wall Street for 30 years have to ask me if it's okay to buy or sell something. I also enjoy the research end. I have found—much to my surprise over the years—that numbers are not intimidating at all. It gives me the opportunity to be both a broker for those clients that I do handle without being compelled to trade in their accounts to make my living. And I like being of assistance to the brokers because, although I don't have a vested interest in whether they buy or sell, over the long term if you do a portfolio structure that is appropriate for their client they keep the client. It's not a question of perhaps buying one or two stocks that don't turn out so the client goes to some other broker. If you can do a total picture so that no single security will make or break them, they're going to keep their portfolio with you.

ADMINISTRATIVE MANAGER, INSTITUTIONAL SALES
MAJOR BROKERAGE FIRM
NEW YORK, NY

My first profession was teaching—I have a B.S. and an M.S. in education—but after three years at the head of a third-grade classroom, I was ready for something new. I was interested in business (and I must admit I was ready to work with adults), but beyond that I didn't have a clear idea of where to start looking. An employment agency sent me to interview for a position as a sales assistant with a brokerage house. I knew little about either securities or sales, but the job interested me and it met my two basic requirements—it didn't require typing and I wouldn't be taking a cut in pay by switching jobs. I didn't get that job, but I found what I had been looking for. I applied for other sales assistant openings and wound up at Thomson McKinnon. That was in 1968.

I learned a great deal about securities. The firm sent me to the New York Institute of Finance, which prepared me to take (and pass) the registered representative exam with the New York Stock Exchange. As I knew I didn't want to be an assistant forever, I pursued sales, moving to a small brokerage house called Hirsch and Company. Few women were in sales at that time. In fact, I have wondered if the primary reason I got that job was because I was interviewed by one of the few female partners then in the business.

I received no formal training—I was given a phone and a desk, and I was on my own! Building a client base was tough. I found myself in a bear market with few products to sell. At the time, brokers dealt mainly with stocks. We sold some bonds, but the options market was really just starting. Today, a broker has much more to work with.

The bad part of being a broker is that you are always on the job. Wherever you go, whomever you meet, one thing is foremost in your mind—making client contacts. I did a lot of cold calling. I did hit on a trick to make contacts, however. I would go through the phone book, calling everyone with my last name. By playing up the coincidence of our names, I could break the ice, and often people would talk to me because of the connection.

The firm went out of business, which gave me a chance to re-evaluate my goals. I came to the conclusion that I would be happier not selling. I was not bad at selling, but the job just didn't fit my personality. I went back to Loeb Rhoades (now a part of Shearson Lehman/American Express), handling day-to-day, administrative details as a supervisor. After four years, I moved to Bache Halsey Stuart, Inc. (now Prudential Bache), where I spent another four years as manager of marketing and support services in the institutional sales department.

In institutional sales, we sell our product—our research—to major clients, such as bank trust departments and large pension funds. I was responsible for discovering what our clients needed in terms of the research itself and what they expected in terms of its presentation. Some wanted a broad analysis; others asked for more specific information. The data must be easily understandable and, above all, must be timely.

I left Bache after four years, moving to my current employer. I still work with institutional sales, but am more involved with overseeing department functions. Institutional sales is now getting into new areas. Electronic transmittal of data is speeding our delivery to customers. We are now looking into closed circuit television. With it, we will be able to contact our clients directly, our research analysts and salespeople won't travel, but may make all their analytical presentations and sales calls on television. Your clients always expect you to have a crystal ball. Not so long ago, clients wanted forecasts for the coming year or two; now they want predictions five years in advance! As research techniques become more sophisticated, our forecasts seem to be getting much more accurate, but of course room for error remains.

Although I do not do actual selling, my sales background has helped me immensely. I understand the pressures on our salespeople. And in a sense, I still do some selling—not to the clients, but to the salespeople. I tell them what we can supply to clients, and I motivate them to sell our services.

I am a member of the Financial Women's Association of New York, an organization that includes women from many different financially oriented professions. I enjoy meeting other professional women to compare notes and exchange information. And, as you progress in your career, networking is important.

INDEX

NOTES

NOTES